BOOKS REMEMBERED:
Nurturing the Budding Writer

Compiled and Edited by
The Children's Book Council

D1195637

The Children's Book Council,Inc. ■ 568 Broadway ■ New York, NY 10012

Editor: Lisa V. Mahmoud

Designer: Jane Byers Bierhorst

Copyright © 1997 by The Children's Book Council, Inc.,
568 Broadway, New York, NY 10012
ISBN: 0-933633-04-1
Manufactured in the United States of America

Cover Illustration: Ted Rand

Alphabetical Guide to Contributing Authors

Note: The articles in this collection appear in the chronological order in which they originally appeared in CBC Features.

Editor's Note

The articles in this collection originally appeared in *The Calendar* or *CBC Features,* publications of the Children's Book Council. The issue in which each remembrance was published is noted at the beginning of each article. The introduction, biographical notes, and bibliographies were especially prepared for this volume.

The bibliographies include both in- and out-of-print titles; first editions only unless a later edition has a new illustrator. In the case of British and Australian authors, both the first British or Australian and first American editions are included. We list only books for children, memoirs, or books about writing for children. Some titles originally written for an adult audience are included if they were also marketed as young adult books.

Many thanks to the authors who provided photographs, brief biographies, and bibliographies. In the case of authors who did not respond to our request for information and those who are deceased, bibliographies were compiled from CHILDREN'S BOOKS IN PRINT, 1969-1997 editions, from TWENTIETH CENTURY CHILDREN'S WRITERS, and from publishers' catalogs. Every attempt was made to make the listings as complete and accurate as possible. Apologies for any omissions or errors.

–Lisa V. Mahmoud
New York City
June 1997

Introduction

Margaret Frith and her
brother Norman

Recently I was browsing in a bookstore when a little girl of about four and her grandparents appeared beside me to look through a low shelf of Beatrix Potter books. The little girl pulled out a copy of THE TALE OF PETER RABBIT and exclaimed that this was the book she wanted. "But," the grandmother said, "you already have this book at home." No matter. This was the book she wanted. Then the grandfather tried, showing her other Potter books. "How about this one, or this?" he asked. She looked at Tom Kitten and Jemima Puddle-Duck, not letting go of Peter. "No," she said quietly. "This one." As I moved on they were still trying to persuade her that she already had this book. But their logic escaped her. What this little girl knew was that she loved *this* book and that was all there was to it.

As I read the wonderful pieces in this collection, some by authors I know personally, and others by those I don't, distinct feelings came to the surface as certain books were mentioned. The one that springs to mind immediately is SARAH CREWE, OR WHAT HAPPENED AT MISS MINCHIN'S (as a child I wondered why this book had two titles). I can see it clearly—a squarish book, a burnished cooper-colored cover with an inset picture in the middle, and black and white line illustrations. I read it over and over again and I was never disappointed. I looked in the bakery window with poor, hungry Sarah; I felt Miss Minchin's wrath; I gloried in the enchantment and safety of her tiny attic room after it was transformed. Bliss!

How lucky I was later in life to be able to publish SARAH CREWE with Margot Tomes. She too loved the story and we decided to do a splendid edition with Margot's full color art, giving it an old-fashioned feeling of plates tipped in. Today I am fortunate to have the jacket and an inside piece, given to me by Margot, hanging on my wall at home, reminding me of childhood and an old friend.

I understood Katherine Paterson's terrified reaction to an illustration for THE LEGEND OF SLEEPY HOLLOW which she saw at too young an age. Sometime my mother must have read THE HOBBIT to my brother and me. He was almost five years older and ready for it and I was not. I don't remember anything about the story or my mother reading it, but I only have to see the cover of the book today, with its deep blue, green and white design, to feel uneasy.

Over time I have listened to the pros and cons discussed as to whether or not children should read only "literature" or be allowed to read "trash" as well. Comic books and series fiction come to mind. I am decidedly on the side of the latter from my own experience. First there was the family next door. My friend Nan and her brother John had the "strict" parents in the neighborhood. They weren't allowed to have comic books so they came to our house to read them. They would walk into town with us on the island of Bermuda where I grew up. A grumpy old man (in our eyes) had a dark cluttered little shop in an alley between Reid Street and Church Street in Hamilton where we bought and sold our comic books.

So I appreciate Laurence Yep's comment that comic books were not a waste of time for him. I agree. I moved easily from comic books; to programs such as "The Shadow" that my brother and I listened to on the radio; to the Saturday morning movies we went to and lapped up the series that came before the main feature; to stories my mother read to us or books we read on our own. All these story forms stimulated my imagination.

I don't remember any bookstores in Bermuda in those days, but there was a library with a children's room. I went there all the time, and I unabashedly confess that the books I first read on my own and loved, like Betsy Byars says in her essay, were series that I could read right through. First I found Enid Blyton, scorned in the field. But I loved those adventures where she always got rid of the parents in the first chapter, and then we were off chasing Nazi spies, a small band of girls and boys, equally sharing in the danger. My favorite was the girl called George, intrepid, smart and brave under fire.

I devoured English boarding school stories with their midnight feasts and I became an avid Nancy Drew fan from watching the ten year old girl next door. How grown up she was, I thought, to be reading Nancy. I was about seven, I think, and much too young for her to have anything to do with me. I couldn't wait to be old enough to read Nancy too.

There were, however, also series that I couldn't stand—Honey Bunch, Pollyanna, and most of all the Elsie Dinsmore books which some relative must have kept giving to me. But those series led me to authors. I found ANNE OF GREEN GABLES and read all of the Anne books. I discovered LITTLE WOMEN and looked for every Louisa May Alcott I could find on the library shelves. Throughout this collection of essays it is the classics that seem to be the common threads, whether the author grew up in America, China, England or Australia. Surely Burnett's THE SECRET GARDEN and Stevenson's TREASURE ISLAND are among the strong favorites. But ROBINSON CRUSOE and THE SWISS FAMILY ROBINSON are up there. What child would not be caught up in those island adventures?

In reading Natalie Babbitt's piece, I was struck with how a single book, both Carroll's words and Tenniel's drawings had an impact on her as a child. ALICE gave her a new view of narrative and illustration, one that charted her course straight into the creation of children's books.

Illustrations can have a strong impact on how the child perceives story. I can picture a copy of THE WATER BABIES in our house. I can remember sitting on the living room floor looking at the illustrations over and over. That underwater world gripped my imagination every time and pulled me in. I would try to read the story, but I never got very far. It wasn't too difficult. It just wasn't for me.

But THE STORY OF FERDINAND THE BULL was, and I pulled it off our shelf over and over again. Russell Freedman's experience of going to buy a copy of FERDINAND as an adult and being disappointed when he found a black and white edition in the store sounded familiar to me. Alice Torrey, editor-in-chief of Coward-McCann, told me a similar story. A man came to her office to complain about Wanda Gág's MILLIONS OF CATS. Why wasn't it published in color anymore as it had been when he was a child? Nothing Alice could say would persuade him that the book he had had as a boy was the same black and white edition. He wouldn't believe that it had never been published any other way. His imagination had seen the story in glorious color and that is how it would remain.

Many of the books mentioned here come from the minds and hearts of storytellers, be they true stories or imagined ones. I never cease to be amazed at an author's ability to remember his or her childhood vividly and fully. Over the years as I have discussed story with authors, they recall experiences in detail as if they happened yesterday. They can make me see and feel as if I had been there with them.

Two authors particularly come to mind—Jean Fritz and Tomie dePaola. How they have each made me laugh and want to hear more. And they have each given more in books right out of their childhoods: Jean's early memories growing up in China in HOMESICK: MY OWN STORY and Tomie's NANA UPSTAIRS, NANA DOWNSTAIRS, one of a number of picture books in which he draws upon his warm family experiences.

My memories are much more fragmented. Instead of picturing detail, I only remember impressions and feelings. For example, when we were young, my brother Norman and I shared a bedroom. A distinct memory is of my mother reading BLACK BEAUTY to us, a chapter a night. I can't hear my mother reading the words, I can only see her there on the bed with my brother and me. I don't remember details of the story. I do remember our suffering with Black Beauty—and our tears

We live in an age when more books than ever are published. Since I entered the field in the early sixties, the output of books for children has more than doubled. Many more books are available for today's children in hardcover and in paperback, the latter a format which most of us in this edition didn't have when we were growing up. The classics remain, but now there is so much more from which to choose.

Who will the authors of tomorrow remember when they are writing for the next generation? I'm certain that books by the authors here will be among those they count among their "books remembered." I'm equally certain that books by the authors here will have the staying power of the classics we all had as children.

We thank you for the books you have given us. We thank you for sharing your memories.

–Margaret Frith
Chairman,
The Putnam & Grosset Group

Pauline Clarke

Vol. 34, No. 1, March-August 1975

A distinguished English author of 27 books for children written between 1948 and 1972, Pauline Clarke has been writing for adults since 1973. Her 1962 classic, THE TWELVE AND THE GENII, published in the U.S. as THE RETURN OF THE TWELVES was awarded the Carnegie Medal, the Deutcsche Jugendbuch Preis, and a place on the Honor List of the International Board on Books for Young People.

When I was young, nothing self-conscious or effortful was done to see we read the right things (compared with what is done by conscientious parents now). My mother in her childhood had simply been made free of all the books she could lay hands on, and probably did not suppose a child needed any other treatment. She saw we had the classics—Alice, Brer Rabbit, Beatrix Potter. Whereas my father was a puritan of strange psychological stamp who regarded reading as suspect because it was pleasurable, and any story about human passion as shameful. So his influence was negative. (In childhood, he would tell us to 'get our heads out of that book'; in adolescence it was necessary to conceal the fact that we were reading JANE EYRE; when I was an adult schoolgirl, he burnt, I always supposed, ALL QUIET ON THE WESTERN FRONT; and fortunately for us both he never caught me reading I, CLAUDIUS.) Perhaps because of these obstacles I wasn't as great, fast or wide a reader as many; and that I've subsequently spent one third (about) of my life writing stories is rather surprising. (Or is it not?) My mother's ardent love of poetry and letters, and the fact that she helped educate her three daughters by a ceaseless stream of stories and articles, no doubt has to do with it.

And the book that moved me most deeply when I was young? A strong candidate is THE WIND IN THE WILLOWS. And if I do not write about it quickly, surely someone else will and I shall have lost the chance. Kenneth Grahame was a sad man, for many reasons; but out of his grief and nostalgia came one of the loveliest of stories. It is, of course, a particularly English book. There is a passionate love of English river country-side in his descriptions of the summer flowers of the river bank, of secret islands, tumbling weirs, mills and fords, snow in the wild wood, moonlight over cornfields. His language, indeed is sometimes poetical to lushness; but as a country child, come from town, I drank this in and it coloured my preferences. Chance sights of rivers winding through meadows still make me want to follow. Then, its main characters are animals, and the English have a special corner in animals. Meeting the Mole, the Rat, the Badger and the Toad increased both my love and perception of animals, and (although I know all the age-old and scientific reasons why they *do*) I *still* cannot bear to hear people hate rats; rats, the most sensitive and highly-organised creatures. To me, they all recall the noble, poetical Water Rat. And this is where Grahame was brilliant: he produced the essential Rat, sensitive to a degree; the essence of Molehood, humble, practical and home-loving; the essential Badger, shy and brusque; the essentially volatile, conceited Toad. (Though in this case the character may well be a 'base libel' on toads, for it is made out of purely physical traits, the creature's ability to leap about and puff itself up, its wide, petulant mouth and staring eyes.) And while he has kept within the proper nature of each animal he has produced real characters whom we immediately recognise, and who are involved with ordinary human beings without a trace of awkwardness, thereby giving his story a place in the long line of animal fables. It has itself produced shoals of inferior imitations, as is often the fate of books of great quality, which only matters if children miss the shining original.

And the story! The marvellous, happy doings of the Mole above ground (once he has wrenched himself from his subterranean spring cleaning), the warmth of the friendship he makes with the Rat, the sensuous satisfactions of those hot river days, with lavish picnics on the grass; or the cosy evenings by the fireside talking and sympathising. It is very much about friendship, its responsibilities and pleasures. How earnestly the Rat, the Mole and the Badger pursue the reformation of Toad (and how often, and comically, he defeats them). With what tact the Rat encourages poor Mole to admit he loves his deserted home despite its narrowness, arranging the marvellous feast for the fieldmice as a celebration. How firmly and kindly the Mole sees to a Rat literally possessed by wanderlust, setting him to scribble poems (very true, this: the only antidote there is to a bad attack). And how loyally both animals join in the search for Otter's lost child. The nonsensical behaviour of Toad provides a good deal of the comedy, his canary-coloured cart and his motor-car, his desperate escape from prison, his exposure by the perspicacious barge-woman, his leap from the engine of the train, his airs and attitudes and childishness. Whereas the humour resides mainly in the delightful interplay between the characters. Menace enters with the subtly described panic terror of the Wild Wood whose cunning and spiteful occupants take over Toad's mansion; and the satisfying climax is the recapture by the four animals, upheld by the comforting strength of the Badger.

Because of the very simplicity of these archetypal patterns, the book has a lasting capacity to touch the heart. What everyone feels about home is there, in the rediscovery of Mole's humble abode. Rat's wander fever, as the wayfarer talks of green seas, distant cities and seething waterfronts, is common to us all. And, not least, every person's sense of the numinous, the mysterious Other greater than we are, is in the vision of the great god Pan, glimpsed with the baby otter asleep between his hooves: Pan, the helper and healer of animals, who causes them quickly to forget pain, trial (and even ecstasy), and to live happily in the everyday.

No wonder A. A. Milne called it, "a Household Book...which everybody...quotes continually ever afterwards". It passed into our conversation: my sisters and I always shared out *à la* Rat: Here's-a-pistol-for-the-Rat, here's-a-pistol-for-the-Mole, here's-a-pistol-for-the-Toad, here's-a-pistol-for-the-Badger. And showed our opinion of the conceited person by a muttered 'Speech, by Toad'.

Bibliography

THE PEKINESE PRINCESS, ill. by Cecil Leslie, Cape, 1948
THE GREAT CAN, ill. by Cecil Leslie, Faber, 1952
THE WHITE ELEPHANT, ill. by Richard Kennedy, Faber, 1952; Abelard-Schuman, 1957
FIVE DOLLS IN A HOUSE (as Helen Clare), ill. by Cecil Leslie, Bodley Head, 1953
MERLIN'S MAGIC (as Helen Clare), ill. by Cecil Leslie, Bodley Head, 1953
SMITH'S HOARD, ill. by Cecil Leslie, Faber, 1955; as HIDDEN GOLD, Abelard-Schuman, 1957; as THE GOLDEN COLLAR, Faber, 1967
SANDY THE SAILOR, ill. by Cecil Leslie, Hamish Hamilton, 1956
THE BOY WITH THE ERPINGHAM HOOD, ill. by Cecil Leslie, Faber, 1956
BEL THE GIANT AND OTHER STORIES (as Helen Clare), ill. by Peggy Fortnum, Bodley Head, 1956; as THE CAT AND THE FIDDLE, AND OTHER STORIES, Prentice Hall, 1967
FIVE DOLLS AND THE MONKEY (as Helen Clare), ill. by Cecil Leslie, Bodley Head, 1956; Prentice Hall, 1967
FIVE DOLLS IN THE SNOW (as Helen Clare), ill. by Cecil Leslie, Bodley Head, 1957; Prentice Hall, 1965
JAMES THE POLICEMAN, ill. by Cecil Leslie, Hamish Hamilton, 1957
JAMES AND THE ROBBERS, ill. by Cecil Leslie, Hamish Hamilton, 1959
TOROLV THE FATHERLESS, ill. by Cecil Leslie, Faber, 1959
FIVE DOLLS AND THEIR FRIENDS (as Helen Clare), ill. by Cecil Leslie, Bodley Head,

1959; Prentice Hall, 1968
SEVEN WHITE PEBBLES (as Helen Clare), ill. by Cynthia Abbott, Bodley Head, 1960
THE LORD OF THE CASTLE, ill. by Cecil Leslie, Hamish Hamilton, 1960
THE ROBIN HOODERS, ill. by Cecil Leslie, Faber, 1960
JAMES AND THE SMUGGLERS, ill. by Cecil Leslie, Hamish Hamilton, 1961
KEEP THE POT BOILING, ill. by Cecil Leslie, Faber, 1961
SILVER BELLS AND COCKLE SHELLS, ill. by Sally Ducksbury, Abelard - Schuman, 1962
THE TWELVE AND THE GENII, ill. by Cecil Leslie, Faber, 1962; as THE RETURN OF THE TWELVES, Coward-McCann, 1964
JAMES AND THE BLACK VAN, ill. by Cecil Leslie, Hamish Hamilton, 1963
FIVE DOLLS AND THE DUKE (as Helen Clare), ill. by Cecil Leslie, Bodley Head, 1963; Prentice Hall, 1968
CROWDS OF CREATURES, ill. by Cecil Leslie, Faber, 1964
THE BONFIRE PARTY, ill. by Cecil Leslie, Hamish Hamilton, 1966
THE TWO FACES OF SILENUS, ill. by Cecil Leslie, Faber; Coward McCann, 1972

Scott O'Dell

Vol. 34, No. 2, September 1975-February 1976

Jim Kalett

*A master of historical fiction for children and
young adults, Scott O'Dell received the Newbery Medal for his
first children's book,* ISLAND OF THE BLUE DOLPHINS *and the
Hans Christian Andersen Medal for the body of his work. In 1981
he established and generously funded the Scott O'Dell Award which is
given annually to a distinguished work of historical fiction.
Mr. O'Dell died in Mount Kisco, New York, in 1989.*

Most of the tales of Hans Christian Andersen and the Brothers Grimm I heard by the time I was four years old. I heard them at dusk, which is the proper time of day to hear fairy tales. I heard them sitting at my mother's knee, which is the best place, the only place to sit when you leave the safe world you know for the unfamiliar and perilous world you don't know.

I heard the Andersen and Grimm stories one each evening—sometimes two if they were short like *Mrs. Gertrude* or *The Goblins*. But without fail, however exciting they were, I always asked for *Jack and the Beanstalk*. My mother must have read it a hundred times. I remember that she would expostulate,"You heard it last night," she'd say, "And the night before and the night before that. I'd think you would get tired of listening." Not me. I sat stolid and silent, certain that she would relent.

And she did. But she began to change events a little—to save her sanity, I presume. Jack would sell a pig instead of a cow, plant morning-glory seeds instead of beans, the castle in the sky might have ten turrets instead of two. But one thing she never dared to change was the verse:

> *Fee, fie, fo, fum!*
> *I smell the blood of an Englishman.*
> *Be he live, or be he dead,*
> *I'll grind his bones to make my bread.*

That was the one that gave me the shivers. To be honest, it still does.

From Jack I graduated to TREASURE ISLAND, to Long John Silver and his wooden leg, two-fingered, tallow-faced Black Dog, the eyeless beggar in the tattered cloak, Bill with a livid saber cut across one cheek and a love for the ditty, "Fifteen Men on a Dead Man's Chest"—a great ditty but not to be compared in the matter of chilling the blood to "Fee, Fie, Fo, Fum."

Over the years, I've read TREASURE ISLAND a dozen times and more, always with pleasure and with undiminished wonder at the opening chapters, more magical by far than any in adventure literature.

It's odd that Stevenson thought so little of TREASURE ISLAND that he published the story under a borrowed name, "Captain George North," and misreading what he had done, burdened it with an uninspired title—THE SEA-COOK. Indeed, he thought so little of TREASURE ISLAND that he criticized England's prime minister for reading it. The great William Gladstone sat up all one night devouring the story and then glowingly passed the word to his friends. Learning of his enthusiasm, Stevenson said that instead of reading TREASURE ISLAND, Gladstone "would do better to attend to the imperial affairs of England."

And there's ROBINSON CRUSOE, which I read a half-dozen times during my childhood—along with SWISS FAMILY ROBINSON. I read it again, many years later, when I started to write ISLAND OF THE BLUE DOLPHINS, to make certain that what I was writing came from my own research and imagination and not Defoe's. A good idea, as it turned out. For one of the dramatic moments in Defoe's story occurs when Robinson Crusoe discovers Friday's footsteps in the sand. One of the dramatic moments in the true story of the Indian girl's eighteen years on the island occurred when the man who rescued her, Captain Nidever, found her footsteps on the beach at Coral Cove. I would have been justified by the facts if I had used this incident. And I debated doing so, but in the end I discarded the idea, for fear of being accused of borrowing.

I don't think there's an age limit on reading. Nor should there be. The emotional area which we share with children is subtle and shadowy. Indeed, in my own life it is not only subtle but at times also interchangeable.

Here's a case in point. A few years ago I stumbled upon a copy of Oscar Wilde's THE HOUSE OF POMEGRANATES in a second-hand bookstore. I had read the stories some fifty years before. But the book was a stylish example of the printer's art. It caught my eye and I took it home, not to read, just to have an attractive book to display on my living-room table.

It was not until a year or so later on a wintry night that, pressed for something to read, I was forced to pick up THE HOUSE OF POME-GRANATES. The book entranced me. And of all of the tales, especially "The Happy Prince."

I like the Prince but even more his dear friend and messenger the Swallow, who wintered in Egypt where a great green snake lived in a palm tree and was fed honey-cakes by twenty priests, and who summered in the north where he fell in love with a river reed:

"'It is a ridiculous attachment,' twittered the other Swallows, 'she has no money, and far too many relations'; and indeed the river was quite full of Reeds."

Many years have passed since "The Happy Prince" was written, dynasties have fallen, fashions have changed. But the tale is still alive, both light-hearted and sad, effortlessly witty and altogether elegant. I enjoyed it then on that wintry night as much as I had long years before.

Bibliography

(All titles published by Houghton Mifflin)

ISLAND OF THE BLUE DOLPHINS, 1960; ill. by Ted Lewin, 1971
THE KING'S FIFTH, ill. by Samuel Bryant, 1966
THE BLACK PEARL, (originally titled THE PEARL OF THE MANTA), ill. by Milton Johnson, 1967
THE DARK CANOE, ill. by Milton Johnson, 1968
JOURNEY TO JERICHO, ill. by Leonard Weisgard, 1969
SING DOWN THE MOON, 1970
THE TREASURE OF TOPO-EL-BAMPO, ill. by Lynd Ward, 1972
THE CRUISE OF THE ARCTIC STAR, ill. by Samuel Bryant, 1973
CHILD OF FIRE, 1974
THE HAWK THAT DARE NOT HUNT BY DAY, 1975
THE 290, 1976
ZIA, ill. by Ted Lewin, 1976
CARLOTA, 1977
KATHLEEN, PLEASE COME HOME, 1978
THE CAPTIVE, 1979
SARAH BISHOP, 1980
THE FEATHERED SERPENT, 1981
THE SPANISH SMILE, 1982
THE AMETHYST RING, 1983
THE CASTLE IN THE SEA, 1983
ALEXANDRA, 1984
THE ROAD TO DAMIETTA, 1985
STREAMS TO THE RIVER, RIVER TO THE SEA: A NOVEL OF SACAGAWEA, 1986

THE SERPENT NEVER SLEEPS: A NOVEL OF JAMESTOWN AND POCAHONTAS, ill.
by Ted Lewin, 1987
BLACK STAR, BRIGHT DAWN, 1988
MY NAME IS NOT ANGELICA, 1989
THUNDER ROLLING IN THE MOUNTAINS, with Elizabeth Hall, 1992

Julia Cunningham

Vol. 35, No. 1, March-August

*Growing up, Julia Cunningham lived in many states before
settling in California, where she helped rebuild a book shop, book
by book. "Writing," she has said, "has brought me much happiness and
certainly the country of the imagination is a wondrous place to be."*

*I*n trying to find my way back to the books that lived in my childhood I
discovered that the journey was really a search for the child. She wasn't
unusual. No Mozart or Daisy Ashford. Her surroundings were bound-
aried with comforts, the kinds that are accepted without much awareness:
a blanketed bed, good food before hunger, a warm house or apartment
wherever the place, parks to play in and a brother to play with and, best of
all, looking backward, an atmosphere of music and books and paints that
encouraged imagination. The how and who of these gifts are not important here. They were, and were as natural as leaf patterns on a summer
wall.

But when she was seven the darkness struck. This was a common psychological darkness caused by the vanishing of a parent but when the night-
mares became frequent and the self-doubts grew weeds in what had surely
been a garden, books began to be more than reasons to laugh or to wonder.
They became what I now believe they are to a multitude of children—res-
cuers, sharers and places to be happy in. I hope my speaking so personally

of the child I was will be understood. She had to be found in order to make sense of her choices.

The first was a story of LITTLE KETTLEHEAD *(out of print)*. This was a gruesome tale of a little girl who played, one day disastrously, with fire. Her head burned off. To hide this disgrace from her parents she painted a face on a kettle and, well concealed by a bonnet, put it on her own neck and went about hoping no one would notice. The book had an implausible and happy ending (Santa Claus gave her a new head) that I never believed. But somehow this horror story helped. I knew how Kettlehead felt and she knew how I felt. Somebody shared.

I regret having SLOVENLY PETER by Heinrich Hoffman *(Warne)* in my memory. I can't to this day forget a page of it. But perhaps it satisfied a need to be punished for that child's secret failures. I think, without a smile, that this book was conceived by an agent of the Devil and most successfully.

My remembering of AT THE BACK OF THE NORTH WIND by George MacDonald *(Dutton)* consists mostly of clouds and diffused light. I think I must have listened to someone reading this book because, having just reread it with awe and love, I seem to hear very distant sounds not unlike the music of a voice. But the vagueness was all a part of a kind of illuminated promise this book gave me. Or perhaps hope is a better word. She, too, that faraway child, might someday arrive at the back of the the North Wind and find answers and simple joy. I never associated it with death but with escape.

THE SECRET GARDEN by Frances H. Burnett *(Lippincott)* gave me friends, safe, uncritical people to be with, and even now I can feel that lovely fall of relaxation as I once read the story over and over. Today, working in a bookstore, I see it bought several times a week and wonder, as a writer, how Mrs. Burnett managed to triumph over a flowery style and reach to the core of so many readers.

Because I had brothers I also loved knights and pirates, kings and queens, dragons and druids, and learned what a hero and a villain were. But these were characters to be enjoyed, acted out and, later, written about in the outside world. I liked being a part of their adventures but the identification was not a deep one.

I don't mean to exclude laughter. It was as necessary as anything and the Oz books led the parade. But I never quite approved of Dorothy. She seemed a little silly to me and it wasn't until, as an adult, I saw Judy Garland in the film that she became a real friend. I believe the genius in Frank Baum would have awarded her a dedication.

And he leads me to the last book, his MAGICAL LAND OF NOOM *(out of print)*. I'm certain that a good critic would dismiss this as a much lesser work than the rest but it taught me, at that first moment of reading and for many years beyond, that there *was* a magic place where one might be free of shadows. All through my life I have glimpsed in certain landscapes a hint of Noom. A particular line of hills or sometimes just intense greenness, as in Ireland, or how grasses rise around a boulder, alert a kind of tiny spring in me and a voice says, "That is like Noom."

Whether it is the child speaking or my present self, I don't know. But I am grateful, as I am for all the unmentioned stories and poems, that books were there for that child to help her cope with and tolerate the darkness that is with everyone and that they were also arrows directing toward the certainty of light.

Bibliography

THE VISION OF FRANÇOIS THE FOX, ill. by Nicolas Angelo, Houghton, 1960
DEAR RAT, ill. by Walter Lorraine, Houghton, 1961
MACAROON, ill. by Evaline Ness, Pantheon, 1962
CANDLE TALES, ill. by Evaline Ness, Pantheon, 1964
DORP DEAD, ill. by James Spanfeller, Pantheon, 1965
VIOLLET, ill. by Alan Cober, Pantheon, 1966
ONION JOURNEY, ill. by Lydia Cooley, Pantheon, 1967
BURNISH ME BRIGHT, ill. by Don Freeman, Pantheon, 1970
WINGS OF THE MORNING, photos by Katy Peake, Golden Gate, 1971
FAR IN THE DAY, ill. by Don Freeman, Pantheon, 1972
THE TREASURE IS THE ROSE, ill. by Judy Graese, Pantheon, 1973
MAYBE, A MOLE, ill. by Cyndy Szekeres, Pantheon, 1974
COME TO THE EDGE, Pantheon, 1977
TUPPENNY, Dutton, 1978
A MOUSE CALLED JUNCTION, ill. by Michael Hague, Pantheon, 1980
FLIGHT OF THE SPARROW, Pantheon, 1980
THE SILENT VOICE, Dutton, 1981
WOLF ROLAND, Pantheon, 1983
OAF, ill. by Peter Sís, Knopf, 1986

Ursula K. Le Guin

Vol. 36, No. 2, November 1977-June 1978

Jill Krementz

Ursula K. Le Guin has received many academic,
popular, and literary awards for her more than forty books of
fiction, poetry, children's stories, and criticism, including a
Newbery Honor for THE TOMBS OF ATUAN. *Her most recent*
books are collections of short stories, FOUR WAYS TO
FORGIVENESS *and* UNLOCKING THE AIR, *and a*
collaborative poetry translation with Diana Bellessi, THE TWINS,
THE DREAM/LAS GEMELAS, EL SUEÑO.

$\mathscr{I}$ am taking this opportunity to try to get in touch with a piece of my childhood that I lost about thirty years ago. I know only the title of the missing piece: THE RISE OF THE RED ALDERS. I have no idea who wrote it. As a child I paid very little attention to authors' names; they were irrelevant; I did not believe in authors. To be perfectly candid, this is still true. I do not believe in authors. A book exists, it's there. The author isn't there—some grownup you never met—may even be dead. The book is what is real. You read it, you and it form a relationship, perhaps a trivial one, perhaps a deep and lasting one. As you read it word by word and page by page, you participate in its creation, just as a cellist playing a Bach suite participates, note by note, in the creation, the coming-to-be, the existence, of the music. And as you read and re-read, the book of course participates in the creation of *you,* your thoughts and feelings, the size and temper of your soul. Where, in all this, does the author come in? Like the God of the eighteenth century deists, only at the beginning. Long ago, before you and the book met each other. The author's work is done, complete; the ongoing work, the present act of creation, is a collaboration by the words that stand on the page and the eyes that read them.

I did, as time went on, discover one modest practical reason for noticing who wrote a book: if I liked one book by this author, I might like another; and authors frequently have the praiseworthy habit of writing more than one book. That was a useful discovery. But I am still bemused by the craving many people have to "know the author"—not only their name, but what they ate for breakfast on April 8, 1934. I can't see the connection. Some authors may indeed be interesting people, who eat interesting breakfasts; that's as may be. But the connection that matters, as I see it, is between the *reader* and the *book.*

A further lapse of time has taught me the second valid reason for noticing the author's name: it's pretty hard to track down a lost, obscure, but beloved book, like THE RISE OF THE RED ALDERS, if you don't know who wrote it. Does anybody out there know? I mobilized the Children's Room of our splendid County Library some years ago, but even they couldn't track it down. I had had some hopes, because as I thought about the book, it seemed to me it might possibly be Oregonian. The red alder is a North West Coast tree, I believe; the main characters of the book are beavers, and Oregon is the Beaver State; and their world, as I recall it, is wet and green and dark and marvelous, like an Oregon forest. But we had no luck.

The Red Alders were not cute beavers with Disney goggle-eyes, nor were they scientifically accurate beavers. They were intelligent, literate beavers with complex emotional lives and—this may be the particular quality of the book—a long, strange history: a mixture of political power struggles and the rise and fall of nations with half-mythicized tribal lore. This element gave, to its reader of ten or so, a vivid, haunting sense of great extents and expanses of time, lived time. It offered, to the mind just leaving the child's nonhistorical and self-centered world, the mystery and lure of other ages, other civilizations. A child may get the first taste of this in books about archaeology, Indians, ancient Egypt or Rome, or in *The National Geographic,* or—all too seldom, in our schools!—in a real history course. I expect many may get it now from THE LORD OF THE RINGS *(Ballantine).* I got it from a book about beavers.

Is it really a good book? I don't know. As I have tried to describe it, it sounds a bit like Richard Adams' WATERSHIP DOWN; but the mood was utterly different, and it was the mood (along with an amiable hero and a good solid plot) that was the beauty of it. It was intense: like a place in the woods, a deep remote stream-gorge, where nobody else ever comes, and where something mysterious happened a long time ago...WATER-SHIP DOWN *(Macmillan)* has those ebullient and inventive rabbit-myths scattered through it, but the tale of the Red Alders *was* a myth. Or so I recall it. As I said, a book is created when it is read; and the amount of creative energy a ten-year-old can put into reading is incredible. We have all made deathless masterpieces out of sows' ears, at ten.

But I don't believe our beavers were sows' ears. I say "our" because my brother Karl was a Red Alder too, and I will never forget the day he came back from Garfield Junior High (I was still in Hillside Elementary) with a grin from ear to ear and, in his hand, O wonder! the sequel!—the book where we could find out what happened to the fascinatingly disgusting villain, a weasel. The sequel is called SKA-DENGE, which means, as I recall, "revenge," in Weasel. The villain left the one word scrawled on a rock at the edge of the boiling river-pit into which he vanished at the end of THE RISE OF THE RED ALDERS. I wish he had also left the author's name, the publisher and date of publication; but really that is too much to ask of a weasel. If there are any people or beavers or anything who read this and can help me, I shall be truly grateful.

Bibliography

A WIZARD OF EARTHSEA, Parnassus, 1968
THE TOMBS OF ATUAN, Atheneum, 1970
THE FARTHEST SHORE, Atheneum, 1972
THE DISPOSSESSED: AN AMBIGUOUS UTOPIA, Harper & Row, 1974
THE WIND'S TWELVE QUARTERS, Harper & Row, 1975
ORSINIAN TALES, Harper & Row, 1976
THE WORD FOR WORLD IS FOREST, Berkley/Putnam, 1976
VERY FAR AWAY FROM ANYWHERE ELSE, Atheneum, 1976
LEESE WEBSTER, ill. by James Brunsman, Atheneum, 1979
COBBLER'S RUNE, ill. by Alicia Austin, Cheap Street, 1983
SOLOMON LEVIATHAN, ill. by Alicia Austin, Philomel, 1988
A VISIT FROM DR. KATZ, ill. by Ann Barrow, Atheneum, 1988
CATWINGS, ill. by S. D. Schindler, Orchard, 1988
CATWINGS RETURN, ill. by S. D. Schindler, Orchard, 1989
FIRE AND STONE, ill. by Laura Marshall, Atheneum, 1989
TEHANU: THE LAST BOOK OF EARTHSEA, Atheneum, 1990
A RIDE ON THE RED MARE'S BACK, ill. by Julie Downing, Orchard, 1992
FISH SOUP, ill. by Patrick Wynne, Atheneum, 1992
WONDERFUL ALEXANDER AND THE CATWINGS, ill. by S. D. Schindler, Orchard, 1994

Natalie Babbitt

Vol. 36, No. 3, July 1978-February 1979

Author/artist Natalie Babbitt has survived twenty-two
different houses in thirteen different towns in seven different states
largely by clinging to one husband, one career, and one editor.
She has made a particular effort not to cling to her children.
Life for her on a scale of one to ten: nine and a half.

To say that they remember ALICE is, for many people, rather like saying they remember their multiplication tables. Words, phrases, verses from both books have been part of the culture for a long time now, popping up in all sorts on unexpected places, and anyone who loved ALICE as a child probably goes back to her every so often, as I do, and finds each time that she is as fresh and sharp as the first time she was encountered.

For me, however, that first time was a kind of revelation and I remember it vividly. For my ninth birthday, my mother had sent away for an edition that contained both ALICEs and THE HUNTING OF THE SNARK. When it arrived, we sat down side by side, unwrapped it (I particularly remember the process of unwrapping) and looked at the pictures together. They seemed to me then, as they do now, a marvel of craftsmanship, strong and crisp and utterly uncondescending, unlike the majority of pictures in my other books, which were either gentle pastels or sternly realistic. That marvel struck me first, though of course I couldn't have articulated it this way then, and was followed closely by the marvel of their funniness. I had never seen, before, pictures that I thought were funny and beautiful at the same time. It had already been decided (prematurely, as it turns out) that I would be an artist when I grew up—my sister was to be the writer—because I spent all of my out-of-school time drawing, but now I knew exactly what kind of artist I wanted to be: an illustrator of children's books, like Tenniel, someone who could create a whole shrewd world with only a pen and black ink.

I should explain here that the year was 1941 and illustration—"commercial art"—was everywhere: on the pages of magazines like *Collier's* and *The Saturday Evening Post* as well as on every available wall and bulletin board in the form of posters dramatizing the War Effort. All of it was full-color and, in one way or another, heavily romantic. I had half-resolved to become a pin-up-girl artist, like Varga in *Esquire,* and had already put a toe into the business by selling my first efforts for 25¢ apiece to other children in the fourth grade. The enterprise was cut off in its infancy by an irate mother—not mine—but the ambition clung until I saw the Tenniel drawings in ALICE. After that, though I still envied Varga's smooth flesh tones—impossible to recreate from a Prang paintbox with its eight little cups of candid color—the clean appeal of black and white established itself as vastly preferable in my imagination. I didn't know then that Tenniel had been a political cartoonist. I didn't recognize Disraeli or any of the other portraits, and didn't realize that the pictures for ALICE were superior in part because they were intelligent. And yet, even now, knowing more, I can't admire those pictures more than I did then.

The two stories, read aloud to me soon after, were another revelation. They actually lived up to the pictures, which was by no means always the case even in 1941. In this particular instance, that meant they were crisp and uncondescending, too, and supremely funny. Imagine—they had no lessons to preach! Quite the contrary. The characters were deliciously rude to one another. They were noisy, they threw things, they cried easily over nothing at all, and they yelled when they were angry. They were allowed simply to be themselves, as richly individual as the pictures had promised, and not a role model in the carload.

One of the discouraging things about most characters in children's stories is that they are so transparent—the heroes so intrepid and resourceful, the bad guys so unredeemably bad. I don't believe children are especially persuaded by this approach—they are far more sophisticated than their literature gives them credit for being. They must, after all, live with *us*. The characters in ALICE, compared to those in PETER PAN or HANS BRINKER or PINOCCHIO, were for me as a child infinitely more familiar and comfortable. And because it was all right to laugh at them, they made the rudeness and bad manners of real people—adults, contemporaries, myself—less appalling. We have all known many Duchesses in our lives, no few by the time we are nine, and just as many White Knights and Caterpillars. ALICE houses the full range of human failings and is as good a guidebook for getting along with one's mates as can be found anywhere. I see this clearly now, but recognized it to a degree even then. And greatly appreciated, especially then, the fact that in ALICE no one—except guinea-pigs—was ever punished for anything.

Some children found—and find—ALICE frightening, but I didn't. The things that happen, the things the characters say, all seemed perfectly logical then and still do. It is not a question of their being consciously explicable, though they have been explained back, forth, and sideways. It is something else—a cast of mind, perhaps. I don't know. But I have loved ALICE as I love few other things—in books or out—and going back to her is every time like going home—not back to Ohio in 1941, but back to myself.

ALICE is entirely responsible for my choosing to labor in the field of children's books. Alas, I did not grow up to be another John Tenniel. Or another Lewis Carroll, either. But that's all right—neither did anybody else. Rich as the field may be these days, it still boasts no one who can match them. There is always something about our butter, by comparison, that doesn't suit the works. I'm glad. I should be very jealous for them otherwise.

Bibliography

(All books were published by Farrar, Straus & Giroux, except where noted. Most are illustrated by the author.)

DICK FOOTE AND THE SHARK, 1967
PHOEBE'S REVOLT, 1968
THE SEARCH FOR DELICIOUS, 1969
KNEEKNOCK RISE, 1970
THE SOMETHING, 1970
GOODY HALL, 1971
THE DEVIL'S STORYBOOK, 1974
TUCK EVERLASTING, 1975
THE EYES OF THE AMARYLLIS, 1977
HERBERT ROWBARGE, 1982
THE DEVIL'S OTHER STORYBOOK, 1987
NELLIE: A CAT ON HER OWN, 1989
BUB—OR THE VERY BEST THING, HarperCollins, 1994

Books by Valerie Worth, illustrated by Natalie Babbitt

SMALL POEMS, 1972
MORE SMALL POEMS, 1976
STILL MORE SMALL POEMS, 1978
CURLICUES, 1979
SMALL POEMS AGAIN, 1986
ALL THE SMALL POEMS AND FOURTEEN MORE, 1994

Joan Aiken

Vol. 37, No. 1, March-October 1979

*Born in Sussex, England, in 1924, a daughter of the
American poet Conrad Aiken, Joan Aiken began writing at age five
and has been at it ever since. Her oeuvre includes novels, plays,
short stories, ghost stories, and verse. She lives in
Sussex and New York and has two children, John and Lizza,
and two grandchildren, Belou and Emil.*

$\mathscr{R}$eading aloud was a daily habit in our family. My mother read aloud to me; she also read to my brother (twelve years older) and to my sister (seven years older). My brother read aloud to my sister; she read aloud to me. My stepfather and my mother read to each other; evening by evening they worked through WAR AND PEACE or the JOURNALS OF ANDRÉ GIDE, or all the Barchester novels. And I, as soon as I was old enough to do so, read aloud to anyone who would listen; my mother and I plugged our way steadily through the Bible, one of us reading and the other slicing beans (or whatever); besides this, all of us would sometimes have Reading Tea; every member of the family was allowed to bring a book to the table and silently munch while turning the pages. And, of course, we all read to my younger brother, who was seven years my junior.

These various threads of reading-aloud made, I now see, a very interesting and comfortable series of extra connections throughout the family. It was as if we all met on a whole system of different interlocking levels: while I was having PINOCCHIO read as a bedtime treat, my elder brother and sister would come and curl up on the end of the bed to listen; and while they were having THE CLOISTER AND THE HEARTH after tea, I would be building with my bricks on the sittingroom floor and listening to *that;* understanding, I suppose less than half of what went on but the half I did understand, wow! what a gripping story!—with its terrific adventures. When I was seven or eight I read it all over again to myself and enjoyed it even more. (Now, re-reading it as an adult, I enjoy it less because I can't help noticing the florid style and remembering the acid comments on it that were passed by my stepfather if he chanced to come into the room during reading period...) And my sister would be reading Dumas for which she must have had quite a passion, for we worked through at least half a dozen, maybe more—all sequels to THE THREE MUSKETEERS, and of course THE COUNT OF MONTE CRISTO and the Marguerite de Valois series. No wonder my sister took to writing historical novels. There was an oubliette in Marguerite de Valois that gave me special pleasure—Catherine de Medici pulled the trapdoor under some unfortunate messenger and then had to go down a thousand winding stairs to retrieve the letter he had refused to hand over to her. Charlotte Yonge's DOVE IN THE EAGLE'S NEST had another terrifying oubliette—oubliettes were rather an obsession with me for a while.

My brother liked to read aloud funny books; it is to him that I owe an early and lasting passion for the short stories of Saki. He also provided the more modern and American element in our family reading, introducing such exotics as Archy and Mehitabel. He read aloud Damon Runyon's stories in a suitably deadpan voice to go with the present-tense narrative form and tough-guy lifestyle; and he read AROUND THE WORLD IN EIGHTY DAYS (*his* passion was for Jules Verne, which perhaps accounts for the high s.f. element in his own novels); he read ghost stories, petrifying us with M. R. James and E. F. Benson (not quite so petrifying, the latter) and books by Bram Stoker, DRACULA and DRACULA'S GUEST.

Looking back I now realize that my mother cunningly practiced the carrot-and-donkey technique in *her* choice of books to read aloud. She would never read us something that we were able to read ourselves. As soon as I had achieved the last page of PETER RABBIT and so was officially declared a reader, my mother read books that would still have been too difficult for me unaided. We went whooshing through OLIVER TWIST— it was so gripping that I can remember taking it on picnics up to the top of the downs, my mother sitting in some wood reading the fearful scene where Oliver thinking himself safe with the kind Maylies, looks out of the window and sees the terrifying figure of Bill Sykes outside. We read A TALE OF TWO CITIES, JANE EYRE, IVANHOE, THE TALISMAN and THE SWISS FAMILY ROBINSON for which I still have a set of crayon illustrations, done when I was six or seven as my mother read it aloud. If I look at them, I can put myself right back into the mood of intense dreamy pleasure that I felt for this splendidly cozy story.

Out of a childhood so layered, so inter-layered with reading, it is hard to pick one favorite book. I loved George MacDonald's Curdie books and still do but I think my final choice for favorite would be two books by Walter de la Mare; I love both so much, I would find it impossible to choose between them. One is his collection of poems, PEACOCK PIE, which fits among my very earliest recollections of being read to in bed on wintry evenings. At age three—two?—I knew half of them by heart.

And the other de la Mare book was a fantasy novel called THE THREE MULLA MULGARS (later reissued by Faber under the title of THE THREE ROYAL MONKEYS). Oh, how I wish I could get a hold of a copy of our original Duckworth edition (1921) with heavenly, mysterious illustrations by Dorothy P. Lathrop catching exactly the spell-binding quality of the story. It is the saga of three monkeys who set off on a quest to look for their lost father. They travel through a forested, mountainous region— India? Arabia?—there are leopards and baboons, elephants and crocodiles—but all is translated into mystery, into fantasy. There are ghosts called Meermuts, a kind of divine being called Tishnar, the representation of all good and beauty; evil and fear are made manifest by a great cat-creature called Immanala. The three heroes make their journey during a kind of supernatural winter, a Fimbulwinter, and they never do get to the end of it. Never mind: by the last page it is plain they are going to reach their destination, and this open ending, or course, filled one's imagination far more than a conventional happy-ever-after would have done.

Is THE THREE MULLA MULGARS as good as I think it? I can't say; for me it still, and completely has the magic it had when it hit me first, somewhere before my fourth birthday.

© 1979 Joan Aiken Enterprises

Bibliography

ALL YOU'VE EVER WANTED, Cape, 1953
MORE THAN YOU BARGAINED FOR, Cape, 1955; Abelard-Schuman, 1957
THE KINGDOM AND THE CAVE, ill. by Victor Ambrus, Abelard-Schuman, 1960; Doubleday, 1974
THE WOLVES OF WILLOUGHBY CHASE, ill. by Pat Marriott, Cape, 1962; Doubleday, 1963
BLACK HEARTS IN BATTERSEA, ill. by Robin Jacques, Cape; Doubleday, 1964
NIGHTBIRDS ON NANTUCKET, ill. by Robin Jacques, Cape; Doubleday, 1966
THE WHISPERING MOUNTAIN, ill. by Frank Bozzo, Cape, 1968; Doubleday, 1969
A NECKLACE OF RAINDROPS, ill. by Jan Pieńkowski, Cape, 1968; Doubleday, 1969
ARMITAGE, ARMITAGE, FLY AWAY HOME, ill. by Betty Fraser, Doubleday, 1968
A SMALL PINCH OF WEATHER, Cape, 1969; Lutterworth, 1988
NIGHT FALL, Macmillan, 1969; Holt, 1970
SMOKE FROM CROMWELL'S TIME, Doubleday, 1970

THE CUCKOO TREE, ill. by Susan Obrant, Cape; Doubleday, 1971
THE KINGDOM UNDER THE SEA AND OTHER STORIES, ill. by Jan Pienkowski, Cape, 1971
THE GREEN FLASH AND OTHER TALES OF HORROR, SUSPENSE AND FANTASY, Holt, 1971
ARABEL'S RAVEN, BBC Paperback, 1972
A HARP OF FISHBONES, Cape, 1972
WINTERTHING: A CHILDREN'S PLAY, ill. by Arvis Stewart, Holt, 1972
DIED ON A RAINY SUNDAY, Gollancz; Holt, 1972
THE ESCAPED BLACK MAMBA, BBC Paperback, 1973
THE MOONCUSSER'S DAUGHTER: A PLAY FOR CHILDREN, ill. by Arvis Stewart, Viking, 1973
MIDNIGHT IS A PLACE, Cape; Viking, 1974
TALES OF ARABEL'S RAVEN, ill. by Quentin Blake, Cape, 1974; as ARABEL'S RAVEN, Doubleday, 1974
THE BREAD BIN, BBC Paperback, 1974
NOT WHAT YOU EXPECTED, ill. by Susan Obrandt, Doubleday, 1974
CASTLE BAREBANE, Gollancz; Viking, 1976
THE SKIN SPINNERS: POEMS, Viking, 1976
MORTIMER'S TIE, BBC Paperback, 1976
A BUNDLE OF NERVES, Gollancz, 1976
THE ANGEL INN, (translated from French), Cape, 1976; Stemmer House, 1978
THE FAR FORESTS: TALES OF ROMANCE, FANTASY AND SUSPENSE, Viking, 1977
THE FAITHLESS LOLLYBIRD, ill. by Eros Keith, Cape, 1977; Doubleday, 1978
GO SADDLE THE SEA, Doubleday, 1977, Cape, 1978
MICE AND MENDELSON, Cape, 1978
TALE OF A ONE-WAY STREET AND OTHER STORIES, ill. by Jan Pieńkowski, Cape, 1978; Doubleday, 1979
STREET: A PLAY, ill. by Arvis Stewart, music by John Sebastian Brown, Viking, 1978
THE SPIRAL STAIR, BBC Paperback, 1979
MORTIMER AND THE SWORD EXCALIBUR, BBC Paperback, 1979
ARABEL AND MORTIMER, ill. by Quentin Blake, BBC/Cape, 1979; Doubleday, 1981
A TOUCH OF CHILL; TALES FOR SLEEPLESS NIGHTS, Gollancz, 1979; Delacorte, 1980
THE SHADOW GUESTS, Cape; Delacorte, 1980; Chivers, 1988
THE STOLEN LAKE, Cape; Delacorte, 1981
MORTIMER'S PORTRAIT ON GLASS, BBC Paperback, 1982
THE MYSTERY OF MR. JONES'S DISAPPEARING TAXI, BBC Paperback, 1982
THE WAY TO WRITE FOR CHILDREN, Elm Tree, 1982
A WHISPER IN THE NIGHT: TALES OF TERROR AND SUSPENSE, Gollancz, 1982; Delacorte, 1984
BRIDLE THE WIND, Cape; Delacorte, 1983
MORTIMER'S CROSS, ill. by Quentin Blake, Cape, 1983; Harper, 1984
THE KITCHEN WARRIORS, BBC Paperback/Knight, 1984
UP THE CHIMNEY DOWN, Cape, 1984; Harper, 1985
FOG HOUNDS, WIND CAT, SEA MICE, Macmillan, 1984
MORTIMER SAYS NOTHING, ill. by Quentin Blake, Cape, 1985; Harper, 1987
THE LAST SLICE OF RAINBOW AND OTHER STORIES, ill. by Alix Berenzy, Cape, 1985; Harper, 1988
PAST EIGHT O'CLOCK, ill. by Jan Pieńkowski, Cape, 1986; Viking, 1987
DIDO AND PA, Cape, 1986; Delacorte, 1987
THE MOON'S REVENGE, ill. by Alan Lee, Cape; Knopf, 1987
THE TEETH OF THE GALE, Cape; Harper, 1988
THE ERL KING'S DAUGHTER, ill. by Paul Warren, Heinemann, 1988; Barron's, 1989
A GOOSE ON YOUR GRAVE, Gollancz, 1987
GIVE YOURSELF A FRIGHT, Delacorte, 1989
A FOOT IN THE GRAVE, Cape; Viking, 1989
VOICES, Hippo, 1988; as RETURN TO HARKEN HOUSE, Delacorte, 1990
A FIT OF SHIVERS, Gollancz, 1990
A CREEPY COMPANY, Gollancz, 1993; Delacorte, 1994
THE WINTER SLEEPWALKER, Cape, 1994
MORTIMER'S MINE, with Lizza Aiken, BBC Paperback, 1994

MORTIMER'S POCKET, with Lizza Aiken, BBC Paperback, 1994
COLD SHOULDER ROAD, Cape, 1995
A HANDFUL OF GOLD, Cape, 1995
MAYHEM IN RUMBURY, BBC Paperback, 1995
THE COCKATRICE BOYS, Gollancz, 1996

Lloyd Alexander

Vol. 38, No. 1, March-October 1981

Alexander Limont

Lloyd Alexander's books have received numerous national and international prizes, including the Newbery Medal for THE HIGH KING *and the National Book Award for* THE MARVELOUS MISADVENTURES OF SEBASTIAN. *Born 30 January 1924, he lives in Drexel Hill, Pennsylvania, with his wife Janine, two cats, and a violin which, he claims, he plays badly.*

Giving one book or author pride of place in my childhood would hurt the feelings of my oldest and dearest friends. Choose Shakespeare and infuriate Dickens. Choose Mark Twain and leave Poe darkly scowling. The Brothers Grimm? Andersen would be cut to the quick. Malory already plucks at my sleeve, Aesop elbows his way through a crowd of Greek mythologists. I loved them all as a boy. I love them still more today. I will not offend a single one of them.

Nevertheless, one book does stand out as my constant companion, comforter, and teacher. I name it now because it includes everything my favorite authors wrote and everything that ever will be written: my dictionary.

I hasten to add: This is not a dictionary but (with echo chamber effect) *A DICTIONARY*. Consider its vital statistics: nine inches by twelve, and nearly a foot thick. Weight: 30 pounds. The pages number 7046 plus a SUPPLEMENT unnumbered, of another couple thousand. Its official title: THE CENTURY DICTIONARY: AN ENCYCLOPEDIC LEXICON OF THE ENGLISH LANGUAGE. Its copyrights run from 1899 to 1914. It is bound in greenish corduroy, iron-hard, coarse-waled, drab but durable. My boyhood knickers surely came from the same bolt of fabric.

This leviathan, this Moby Dick of dictionaries weighs down the floor beside my work table as I write these words. When my wife and I first set up housekeeping, I brought it from my parents' storage closet. Last night, trying to set my thoughts in order, I went rummaging for it among the oddments in our attic—in itself a perilous quest, like crawling into some giant's game of jackstraws—and hauled it down, to the dismay of my sacroiliac. I had not consulted it for years, having been seduced by slimmer, more up-to-date volumes. Up-to-date is all well and good; but this is an ancestor, an archetype. In addition to defining unfamiliar words, my dictionary served other purposes. For one, I read it when nothing else was available; one entry leading to another in a fascinating chain of associations. The illustrations alone offered a lifetime of study. I still haven't seen all of them, though I have just now glanced at meticulously detailed cuts of bargeboard construction, the conirostral bill of the hawfinch, and the obverse and reverse sides of a Louis XIV jetton (actual size).

For another, I often sat on it, while reading other books, and thus had a ready reference immediately, as it were, at hand. It was an object of prurient interest when I grew old enough to be interested in prurience. It held all the forbidden words; most of them, regrettably, so forbidden I didn't know what they were and therefore couldn't look them up. But I knew they must be in there, and that was titillating enough.

It served, also, as a filing cabinet. Here I find, tucked between pages 650 and 651, a newspaper advertisement offering a free phonograph record in exchange for a specified number of coupons. Evidently, I never took advantage of the opportunity. On the other side, the fragment of an AP dispatch: *"In the Warsaw raids the suburbs were the heaviest sufferers....Poland's armies, it was asserted authoritatively, are everywhere stemming the invasion..."* The paper, at that point, is torn.

Here, inserted at "J," is a snapshot of a boyhood friend, Jones (first name Alan, never called anything but Jones), peering intently into my camera lens (photography was, briefly, a hobby). Probably a genius, certainly a polymath, an excellent pianist, a linguist, planning to be a zoologist, he introduced me to Goethe, Schiller, and Lessing. He was killed in the Battle of the Bulge.

Under "R," a snapshot taken that same year; Rusty, another close friend, walking briskly out of the schoolyard. His parents had a real library, unlike mine. He let me borrow a book that was, so he had heard, utterly wicked. "It's about a—a *bastard*," he whispered, hardly daring to pronounce the word, as I hardly dared to listen to it. I began reading it secretly:

"An author ought to consider himself, not as a gentleman who gives a private or eleemosynary treat (to the dictionary for "eleemosynary") *but rather as one who keeps a public ordinary."*

An unpromising beginning, I skipped to find the good parts, discovered none, and gave up. I read it twenty years later and count it now among the books I love best.

Here, at "P," comes a treasure: half a dozen small flowers pressed between sheets of waxed paper. I was, at the time, devoted to THE SCARLET PIMPERNEL. One of my eccentricities was to eat, if possible, whatever foods were mentioned in the book I was reading. In this case, I wanted the emblem itself. After long questing, I found a seedsman who sold me a packet of *Anagallis arvensis*. I planted the seeds in our backyard and they actually grew: faded now to pale pink, the blossoms were indeed scarlet.

A central mystery remains, and no one is alive to solve it for me. The dictionary was mine only by squatter's rights. Who acquired it in the first place? My parents, inveterate nonreaders, bought books only at my desperate urging. Who, then? Not my grandmother, who kept a sort of rooming house for near and distant relatives, a way station on the way to another way station; a place where some aged cousin might come, finally to die. Perhaps my Aunt Annie, frail, always in long black skirts, a retired schoolmistress and librarian. A permanent lodger, she had her own marvelous collection of books and read to me whenever I visited, paying no attention to the radio static, the endless talk of money lacking, of dental problems, gall bladders, bankruptcies, obscure lawsuits (as plaintiff or defendant, I never knew).

Literary reminiscence should be elegant; the cosy fireside, the parental lap, the Proustian madeleine. "What a piece of work is a man!" my aunt would recite to me. "How noble in reason! In action how like an angel, in apprehension how like a god..." while an uncle gargled with Lavoris, coughing his lungs out in a back bedroom. Throughout my childhood, knowing nothing different, I took all this as quite normal: confusion, disorder, gossip about quarrels, infidelities, separations; tears, sudden deaths, bursts of laughter, funerals, the arrival of a bawling infant (whose, I have no idea). Older, visiting other families, observing how sensible people lived enviable, well-ordered lives, I was retroactively embarrassed, half-ashamed. I, wishing to be a writer—how could I hope to write anything, with my life such an appalling mess?

Much later, I understood how lucky I was.

Bibliography

The Prydain Chronicles

THE BOOK OF THREE, Holt, 1964
THE BLACK CAULDRON, Holt, 1965
THE CASTLE OF LLYR, Holt, 1966
TARAN WANDERER, Holt, 1967
THE HIGH KING, Holt, 1968
THE FOUNDLING, ill. by Margot Zemach, Holt, 1973

The Westmark Trilogy

WESTMARK, Dutton, 1981
THE KESTREL, Dutton, 1982
THE BEGGAR QUEEN, Dutton, 1984

The Vesper Holly Adventures

THE ILLYRIAN ADVENTURE, Dutton, 1986
THE EL DORADO ADVENTURE, Dutton, 1987
THE DRACKENBERG ADVENTURE, Dutton, 1988
THE JEDERA ADVENTURE, Dutton, 1989
THE PHILADELPHIA ADVENTURE, Dutton, 1990

Other Books for Young People

BORDER HAWK, ill. by Bernard Krigstein, Farrar, 1958
THE FLAGSHIP HOPE, ill. by Bernard Krigstein, Farrar, 1960
TIME CAT, ill. by Bill Sokol, Holt, 1963
COLL AND HIS WHITE PIG, ill. by Evaline Ness, Holt, 1965
THE TRUTHFUL HARP, ill. by Evaline Ness, Holt, 1967
THE MARVELOUS MISADVENTURES OF SEBASTIAN, Dutton, 1970
THE KING'S FOUNTAIN, ill. by Ezra Jack Keats, Dutton, 1971
THE FOUR DONKEYS, ill. by Lester Abrams, Holt, 1972
THE CAT WHO WISHED TO BE A MAN, Dutton, 1973
THE WIZARD IN THE TREE, ill. by Laszlo Kubinyi, Dutton, 1975
THE TOWN CATS, ill. by Laszlo Kubinyi, Dutton, 1977
THE FIRST TWO LIVES OF LUKAS-KASHA, Dutton, 1978
THE REMARKABLE JOURNEY OF PRINCE JEN, Dutton, 1991
THE FORTUNE-TELLERS, ill. by Trina Schart Hyman, Dutton, 1992
THE ARKADIANS, Dutton, 1995
THE HOUSE OF GOBBALEEN, ill. by Diane Goode, Dutton, 1995
THE IRON RING, Dutton, 1997
THE FIRST TWO LIVES OF LUKAS-KASHA, Dutton, 1978
THE REMARKABLE JOURNEY OF PRINCE JEN, Dutton, 1991
THE FORTUNE-TELLERS, ill. by Trina Schart Hyman, Dutton, 1992
THE ARKADIANS, Dutton, 1995
THE HOUSE OF GOBBALEEN, ill. by Diane Goode, Dutton, 1995
THE IRON RING, Dutton, 1997

Beverly Cleary

Vol. 38, No. 3, July 1982-February 1983

Edis Jurcys Photography

*Beverly Cleary has delighted young readers
with her true-to-life tales since the 1950s and her books
continue to garner numerous children's choice awards. She was
awarded the Newbery Medal for* DEAR MR. HENSHAW
*and the Laura Ingalls Wilder Award for her "substantial and
lasting contribution to literature for children."
Ms. Cleary lives in Carmel, California.*

*M*y first experience with a book was fraught with peril. When I was four years old and lived on a farm outside Yamhill, Oregon, a neighbor showed me a picture book which so delighted me that she invited me to look at it any time I pleased. Unfortunately her bachelor son had made a deal to sell me for a nickel to another neighbor, Quong Hop, who was planning to return to China to die. To reach the book I had to pass Quong Hop's house, and since I did not want to go to China, but I did want to see that book, I snaked on my stomach through tall grass and arrived damp with spitbug spit. Alert for the son's footsteps so I could hide in the pantry, I perched on a kitchen chair and studied the pictures of red-coated men on horseback chasing a fox with a pack of hounds. At the end of the book they held the fox's tail triumphantly aloft. Fascinating! Nothing like this went on in Yamhill. The crawl home left me even damper with spitbug spit and longing for more books.

Books required less courage after my mother organized a library stocked with books shipped from the State Library. Jacob's MORE ENG-LISH FAIRY TALES was so precious because of the gruesome little tale of the Hobyahs that my mother had to pry the book from my fingers at bed-time. There were other treasures—Andrew Lang's collections, JOHNNY CROW'S GARDEN, the books of Beatrix Potter, especially THE TAILOR OF GLOUCESTER with its picture of the beautiful crewelwork waistcoat and the tiny note, "No more twist." (I took up needlework about that time.) Innocently unaware that THE STORY OF LITTLE BLACK SAMBO was offensive to anyone, I cherished that tiny red book because it was about a *child,* the first child I had met in a story. That brave little boy with loving parents was my friend.

If Oregon in the 1920's was a literary colony of the British Empire, my reader, when we moved to Portland and I entered a frightening place called school, was one of Britain's outposts. I resented its version of LITTLE GOODY TWO SHOES, for it said that when Goody wished to learn to read, she borrowed a book, sat down and "read and read" without revealing to me how she was able to do this. Goody then tripped about her village with a basket of letters teaching children to read, which sounded easy when I was so miserable. At the end of the story when Sir Charles married Goody in a "great church," my reader asked, "Do you think she deserved to be happy?" Filled with dark, despairing thoughts, I answered, "Shut up, book." Why couldn't I read real books like THE PRINCESS AND CUR-DIE and all the other good books my mother read aloud?

The discovery of the gentle humor and easy style of the twin series by Lucy Fitch Perkins saved me by showing me I really could read. After whizzing through the series, I turned to fairy tales, the joy of my child-hood. On the front steps in summer and with my feet over the furnace outlet in winter, I read, loving those dark smelly buckram bindings which meant others had read the books and now I could, too. I am sure I read every book of fairy tales in our branch library, with only one complaint—all that long golden hair. Never mind—my short brown hair became long and golden as I read, and when I grew up I would write a book about a brown-haired girl to even things up.

While my mother read aloud to my father and me myths, travel books and every funny story she could find, usually from *The Saturday Evening Post,* I plucked fiction for my own reading from the library shelves, reading and rereading all the classics of the time—PINOCCHIO, HEIDI, THE SECRET GARDEN, SWISS FAMILY ROBINSON, HANS BRINKER and others—as well as bound volumes of ST. NICHOLAS. Like the mid-dle Moffat, I began with Alcott and resolved to read straight through to Zwilgmeyer. Did Janie Moffat, I wonder, begin to skip when she reached Altsheler? One book I refused to open, THE BASTABLE CHILDREN, a bulky pea-green anthology of E. Nesbit stories. I thought Bastable meant bastard, to me another word for orphan, and I felt fiction was overpopulated with orphans. An only child, I wanted to read about families. If a book was about a family, I read it even though I did not like it, THE FIVE LITTLE PEPPERS being at the top of my list of disliked books. To this day I save and reuse basting threads because the goody-goody little Peppers did.

Years later, when I received my first royalty check, I thought of the books of my childhood and of the two that had meant the most. Because I felt I owed each author—or her estate—a royalty for the pleasure she had given me, I bought DANDELION COTTAGE by Carol Watson Rankin and DOWNRIGHT DENCEY by Caroline Dale Snedeker. Both books, after a life of about fifty years, are now out of print.

DANDELION COTTAGE does not hold up by today's standards. The small town setting and the adult characters now seem trite, the writing a bit stilted and parts of the plot contrived, and yet the story of four very real girls who were allowed to use a rundown parsonage for a playhouse was right for me when I was in the fourth grade because it was what I wanted to read most—a humorous story about children playing together. If only I had understood that Bastable was a name and not an adjective!

DOWNRIGHT DENCEY, a 1928 Newbery Honor Book, seems as fresh to me as when I first read it. Dencey, a stubborn, conscientious Quaker girl in 19th century Nantucket who rebelled against her mother by befriending a foundling boy and teaching him to read, stirred the sympathy of a conscientious Oregonian who was beginning to feel rebellious. Best of all, here was an author who understood how children behaved when they struggled to read. This book was my bridge to adult books because it followed Dencey from childhood into adolescence, the love of her parents for one another was woven into the story, and because all the adult characters were alive and real.

JANE EYRE came next, and about that time my class was presented with adult library cards along with our eighth grade diplomas. I was proud of that adult card and all it stood for, but from time to time I slipped back to the children's shelves of the library to visit old friends. I still do.

Bibliography

(All titles published by Morrow Junior Books)

Middle readers

BEEZUS AND RAMONA, ill. by Louis Darling, 1955
RAMONA THE PEST, ill. by Louis Darling, 1968
RAMONA THE BRAVE, ill. by Alan Tiegreen, 1975
RAMONA AND HER FATHER, ill. by Alan Tiegreen, 1977
RAMONA AND HER MOTHER, ill. by Alan Tiegreen, 1979
RAMONA QUIMBY, AGE 8, ill. by Alan Tiegreen, 1981
RAMONA FOREVER, ill. by Alan Tiegreen, 1984

THE MOUSE AND THE MOTORCYCLE, ill. by Louis Darling, 1965
RUNAWAY RALPH, ill. by Louis Darling, 1970
RALPH S. MOUSE, ill. by Paul O. Zelinsky, 1982

HENRY HUGGINS, ill. by Louis Darling, 1950
HENRY AND BEEZUS, ill. by Louis Darling, 1952
HENRY AND RIBSY, ill. by Louis Darling, 1954
HENRY AND THE PAPER ROUTE, ill. by Louis Darling, 1957
HENRY AND THE CLUBHOUSE, ill. by Louis Darling, 1962
RIBSY, ill. by Louis Darling, 1964

ELLEN TEBBITS, ill. by Louis Darling, 1951
OTIS SPOFFORD, ill. by Louis Darling, 1953
EMILY'S RUNAWAY IMAGINATION, ill. by Beth and Joe Krush, 1961
MITCH AND AMY, ill. by George Porter, 1967; ill. by Bob Marstall, 1991
SOCKS, ill. by Beatrice Darwin, 1973
DEAR MR. HENSHAW, ill. by Paul O. Zelinsky, 1983
LUCKY CHUCK, ill. by J. Winslow Higginbottom, 1984
MUGGIE MAGGIE, ill. by Kay Life, 1990
STRIDER, ill. by Paul O. Zelinsky, 1991

Picture Books

THE REAL HOLE, ill. by Mary Stevens, 1960; ill. by DyAnne DiSalvo-Ryan, 1986
TWO DOG BISCUITS, ill. by Mary Stevens, 1961; ill. by DyAnne DiSalvo-Ryan, 1986
JANET'S THINGAMAJIGS, ill. by DyAnne DiSalvo-Ryan, 1987
THE GROWING-UP FEET, ill. by DyAnne DiSalvo-Ryan, 1987
PETEY'S BEDTIME STORY, ill. by David Small, 1993

Older readers

FIFTEEN, ill. by Beth and Joe Krush, 1956
THE LUCKIEST GIRL, 1958
JEAN AND JOHNNY, ill. by Beth and Joe Krush, 1959
SISTER OF THE BRIDE, ill. by Beth and Joe Krush, 1963

Memoirs

A GIRL FROM YAMHILL, 1988
MY OWN TWO FEET, 1995

Myra Cohn Livingston

Vol. 39, No. 1, March-October 1983

Myra Cohn Livingston
and her sister Hannah

M. L. Cohn

*Myra Cohn Livingston was widely known and respected
as a poet, anthologist, lecturer, and teacher. Whether writing about
childhood or social issues, she believed poetry was of vital importance.
A recipient of the National Council of Teachers of English
Award for Excellence in Poetry for Children and numerous other
awards and honors, Ms. Livingston lived in
Beverly Hills, California, until her death in 1996.*

The books are remembered not by title alone. They are part of the tall, walnut bookshelves in my parents' living room, a small oak bookcase in my grandmother's upstairs hall, the shelves recessed in stucco behind grillwork of black wrought iron in my aunt's home and cubbyholes in a blue desk in the attic. Each has its place, its individual shape, color, binding and mood. Some are mingled with the sound of my mother's voice, the feel of the paper, the variations of type, the illustrations that even now recall seasons and place, a climate of the mind and hour. Some echo with the sound of rain, a distant train whistle, the wakefulness of a mourning dove; others recall the fragrance of lilac or the Christmas tree.

There was always poetry. At three, I was bedridden for months with rheumatic fever. How many hours must Mother have read to me from

Christina Rossetti's SING SONG, a small book bound in green with its verses that asked the first unanswerable question—"Who has seen the wind?" There was SPIN TOP SPIN with the muted pastels of strange looking children: "Spin top, spin/Where has Peter gone?"—a haunting line that reverberated with the same wonder as "Over the hills and a long way off" in THE REAL MOTHER GOOSE with its oversized stiff pictures. Most mysterious of all was a large, thin book with pages of brown, TAN-DARADEI. Mother had studied German and would read:

> *Im garten in der Morgenfrüh,*
> *Tandari-darei!*
> *Da tanzt der Hans und die Marie*
> *Im schönen Monat Mai.*
> *Eiasusu!*
> *Wir beide, ich und du!*
> *Ein kleiner ogel Quinkirilüt,*
> *Der macht Music dazu.*

Eiasusu! A call to another world far from Omaha, Nebraska, lived in those books, a world that began in the underground of WHEN THE ROOT CHILDREN WAKE UP to the Budapest of the Petersham's MIKI. I could understand the grim grandfather of AUNTIE who sat in a huge chair much as my own grandfather, but Miki slept under the Milky Way with sheepherders, warmed himself against a clay stove, danced in white pants fringed with red and slept in a bed of huge multicolored pillows. Warmth and joy lived in those pages surrounded by patterned borders, whereas even the slick pages of Andersen's THE SNOW QUEEN seemed chilled with the ice and cruelty of the evil that separated Kay and Gerda. This was the book I carried to a "library" created by my fourth grade teacher, a single shelf that held at most a dozen books, loaned by classmates. It was here that I met ONE HUNDRED BEST POEMS FOR BOYS AND GIRLS, a book with coarse paper and dull cover with silhouettes ugly by contrast to my books at home, a book that did not conjure up the "Windy Nights" of Robert Louis Stevenson's horseman or Robert Browning's Pied Piper.

For I remember, as well, the books I would not read. They stood stiffly on shelves, in friends' homes, all the same size, uniform and dull, in green and pink, THE FIVE LITTLE PEPPERS, THE LITTLE COLONEL series. The bindings of the Oz books intrigued me, but the words within did not ring with the rhythms of the poetry I heard in Tennyson's songs from THE PRINCESS, in Walter de la Mare. On a low shelf at home there was one two-volume set with covers of glassine, bound in a beautiful blue. I opened them countless times to look at the pictures, but the child within seemed strange and alien—Alice, falling into a rabbit hole or going through a looking glass. Did the vague unrest, perhaps even fear, arise from the thought that Alice had to go it alone, that those she met were rude and frightening? Or was I too serious a child? I did not read ALICE until I reached college.

Laughter abounded in H.G. Wells' THE ADVENTURES OF TOMMY, and PINOCCHIO, a thick volume with the intriguing Mussino illustrations. In THE ADVENTURES OF DRUSILLA DOLL I found proof that my dolls did, indeed, lead a midnight life without me. But the book from which I would learn to read was a handsome, almost ethereal volume with pale yellow boards, a dust jacket of white tissue, a spine smooth and white to the touch. The fragile pastels of Millicent Sowerby introduced me not only to the story of CINDERELLA but to the look and feel of beautiful thick paper from which arose a haunting perfume that may have been ink, paper or glue; I do not know to this day. But each time I opened it the beauty enveloped me. I had other versions of CINDEREL-LA, but the mood lived only in that book.

Winter was a time for dreaming; an escape to a hut where Snow White and Rose Red patted a bear in a small cottage, where Nutcracker and Sugar Dolly fell in love on Christmas Eve, where children sang NURSERY SONGS FROM FRANCE and danced on the bridge at Avignon and Oscar Wilde's THE SELFISH GIANT turned a garden to white. Summer books came later in my grandmother's house, the lives of POLLYANNA, DEAR ENEMY, MRS. WIGGS OF THE CABBAGE PATCH and EMILY OF THE NEW MOON. But these I read with my head and not my heart. The words have never remained with me.

The books are remembered for their dreams, many realized, many lost with childhood. I have seen the grandeur of Mt. St. Michel beyond the power of any illustrator to capture and the changing of the guards at Buckingham Palace. But over the hills, far away, still stands the Great Sphinx and Budapest. Where Peter has gone is the secret of the unseen wind.

What I remember, most of all, is the difference that beautiful books can make in a life; a tradition still carried on by many; a tradition which I hope will never cease for the young, whose passion for books may ever spawn new dreams.

Bibliography

WHISPERS AND OTHER POEMS, ill. by Jacqueline Chwast, Harcourt, 1958
WIDE AWAKE AND OTHER POEMS, ill. by Jacqueline Chwast, Harcourt, 1959
I'M HIDING, ill. by Erik Blegvad, Harcourt, 1961
I TALK TO ELEPHANTS!, photos by Isabel Gordon, Harcourt, 1962
SEE WHAT I FOUND, ill. by Erik Blegvad, Harcourt, 1962
I'M NOT ME, ill. by Erik Blegvad, Harcourt, 1963
HAPPY BIRTHDAY, ill. by Erik Blegvad, Harcourt, 1964
THE MOON AND A STAR AND OTHER POEMS, ill. by Judith Shahn, Harcourt, 1965
I'M WAITING, ill. by Erik Blegvad, Harcourt, 1966
OLD MRS. TWINDLYTART AND OTHER RHYMES, ill. by Enrico Arno, Harcourt, 1967

A TUNE BEYOND US: A COLLECTION OF POETRY*, ill. by James J. Spanfeller, Harcourt, 1968
A CRAZY FLIGHT AND OTHER POEMS*, ill. by James J. Spanfeller, Harcourt, 1969
SPEAK ROUGHLY TO YOUR LITTLE BOY: A COLLECTION OF PARODIES AND BUR-LESQUES, TOGETHER WITH THE ORIGINAL POEMS, CHOSEN AND ANNOTATED FOR YOUNG PEOPLE*, ill. by Joseph Low, Harcourt, 1971
LISTEN, CHILDREN, LISTEN: AN ANTHOLOGY OF POEMS FOR THE VERY YOUNG*, ill. by Trina Schart Hyman, Harcourt, 1972
THE MALIBU AND OTHER POEMS, ill. by James Spanfeller, McElderry, 1972
THE POEMS OF LEWIS CARROLL*, ill. by John Tenniel, et al., Crowell, 1973
WHAT A WONDERFUL BIRD THE FROG ARE: AN ASSORTMENT OF HUMOROUS POETRY AND VERSE*, Harcourt, 1973
WHEN YOU ARE ALONE/IT KEEPS YOU CAPONE: AN APPROACH TO CREATIVE WRITING WITH CHILDREN, Atheneum, 1973
COME AWAY, ill. by Irene Haas, McElderry, 1974
THE WAY THINGS ARE AND OTHER POEMS, ill. by Jenni Oliver, McElderry, 1974
ONE LITTLE ROOM, AN EVERYWHERE: POEMS OF LOVE*, ill. by Antonio Frasconi, McElderry, 1975
4-WAY STOP AND OTHER POEMS, ill. by James Spanfeller, McElderry, 1976
O FRABJOUS DAY: POETRY FOR HOLIDAYS AND SPECIAL OCCASIONS*, McElderry, 1976
CALLOOH! CALLAY! HOLIDAY POEMS FOR YOUNG READERS*, ill. by Janet Stevens, McElderry, 1978
A LOLLYGAG OF LIMERICKS, ill. by Joseph Low, McElderry, 1978
O SLIVER OF LIVER, TOGETHER WITH OTHER TRIOLETS, CINQUAINS, HAIKU, VERSES, AND A DASH OF POEMS, ill. by Iris Van Rynbach, McElderry, 1979
NO WAY OF KNOWING: DALLAS POEMS, McElderry, 1980
POEMS OF CHRISTMAS*, McElderry, 1980
A CIRCLE OF SEASONS, ill. by Leonard Everett Fisher, Holiday House, 1982
HOW PLEASANT TO KNOW MR. LEAR! EDWARD LEAR'S SELECTED WORKS*, Holiday House, 1982
WHY AM I GROWN SO COLD: POEMS OF THE UNKNOWABLE*, McElderry, 1982
CHRISTMAS POEMS*, ill. by Trina Schart Hyman, Holiday House, 1984
MONKEY PUZZLE AND OTHER POEMS, ill. by Antonio Frasconi, McElderry, 1984
SKY SONGS, ill. by Leonard Everett Fisher, Holiday House, 1984
A SONG I SANG TO YOU: A SELECTION OF POEMS, ill. by Margot Tomes, Harcourt, 1984
THE SCOTT FORESMAN ANTHOLOGY OF CHILDREN'S LITERATURE*, with Zena Sutherland, Scott Foresman, 1984
CELEBRATIONS, ill. by Leonard Everett Fisher, Holiday House, 1985
EASTER POEMS*, ill. by John Wallner, Holiday House, 1985
A LEARICAL LEXICON: A MAGNIFICENT FEAST OF BOSHBLOBBERBOSH AND FUN FROM THE WORKS OF EDWARD LEAR*, ill. by Joseph Low, McElderry, 1985
THANKSGIVING POEMS*, ill. by Stephen Gammell, Holiday House, 1985
WORLDS I KNOW AND OTHER POEMS, ill. by Tim Arnold, McElderry, 1985
EARTH SONGS, ill. by Leonard Everett Fisher, Holiday House, 1986
HIGGLEDY-PIGGLEDY: VERSES AND PICTURES, ill. by Peter Sís, McElderry, 1986
POEMS FOR JEWISH HOLIDAYS*, ill. by Lloyd Bloom, Holiday House, 1986
SEA SONGS, ill. by Leonard Everett Fisher, Holiday House, 1986
CAT POEMS*, ill. by Trina Schart Hyman, Holiday House, 1987
I LIKE YOU, IF YOU LIKE ME: POEMS OF FRIENDSHIP*, McElderry, 1987
NEW YEAR'S POEMS*, ill. by Margot Tomes, Holiday House, 1987
THESE SMALL STONES*, with Norma Faber, Harper, 1987
VALENTINE POEMS*, ill. by Patience Brewster, Holiday House, 1987
POEMS FOR MOTHERS*, ill. by Deborah Kogan Ray, Holiday House, 1988
SPACE SONGS, ill. by Leonard Everett Fisher, Holiday House, 1988
THERE WAS A PLACE AND OTHER POEMS, McElderry, 1988
BIRTHDAY POEMS, ill. by Margot Tomes, Holiday House, 1989
DILLY DILLY PICCALILLI: POEMS FOR THE VERY YOUNG*, ill. by Eileen Christelow, McElderry, 1989
HALLOWEEN POEMS*, ill. by Stephen Gammell, Holiday House, 1989

POEMS FOR FATHERS*, ill. by Robert Casilla, Holiday House, 1989
REMEMBERING AND OTHER POEMS, McElderry, 1989
UP IN THE AIR, ill. by Leonard Everett Fisher, Holiday House, 1989
DOG POEMS*, ill. by Leslie Morrill, Holiday House, 1990
IF THE OWL CALLS AGAIN: A COLLECTION OF OWL POEMS*, ill. by Antonio Frasconi, McElderry, 1990
MY HEAD IS RED AND OTHER RIDDLE RHYMES, ill. by Tere LoPrete, Holiday House, 1990
POEMS FOR GRANDMOTHERS*, ill. by Patricia Cullen-Clark, Holiday House, 1990
LOTS OF LIMERICKS*, ill. by Rebecca Perry, McElderry, 1991
POEMS FOR BROTHERS, POEMS FOR SISTERS*, ill. by Jean Zallinger, Holiday House, 1991
POEM-MAKING: WAYS TO BEGIN WRITING POETRY, HarperCollins, 1991
I NEVER TOLD AND OTHER POEMS, McElderry, 1992
IF YOU EVER MEET A WHALE: POEMS*, ill. by Leonard Everett Fisher, Holiday House, 1992
LET FREEDOM RING: A BALLAD OF MARTIN LUTHER KING, JR., ill. by Samuel Byrd, Holiday House, 1992
LIGHT AND SHADOW, photos by Barbara Rogasky, Holiday House, 1992
A TIME TO TALK: POEMS OF FRIENDSHIP*, ill. by Brian Pinkney, McElderry, 1992
ABRAHAM LINCOLN: A MAN FOR ALL THE PEOPLE: A BALLAD, ill. by Samuel Byrd, Holiday House, 1993
ROLL ALONG: POEMS ON WHEELS*, McElderry, 1993
ANIMAL, VEGETABLE, MINERAL: POEMS ABOUT SMALL THINGS*, ill. by Vincent Nasta, HarperCollins, 1994
FLIGHTS OF FANCY AND OTHER POEMS, McElderry, 1994
KEEP ON SINGING: A BALLAD OF MARIAN ANDERSON, ill. by Samuel Byrd, Holiday House, 1994
PLATERO Y YO/PLATERO AND I, as translator with Juan Ramon Jiménez, ill. by Antonio Frasconi, Clarion, 1994
RIDDLE-ME RHYMES*, ill. by Rebecca Perry, McElderry, 1994
CALL DOWN THE MOON: POEMS OF MUSIC*, McElderry, 1995
B IS FOR BABY: AN ALPHABET OF VERSES, photos by Steel Stillman, McElderry, 1996
FESTIVALS, ill. by Leonard Everett Fisher, Holiday House, 1996

* anthology or collection

E. L. Konigsburg

Vol. 39, No. 3, October 1984-July 1985

E. L. Konigsburg is the only author
to date who has won a Newbery Honor and a Newbery Medal
in the same year, 1968, for her first two novels.
Her recent novel, THE VIEW FROM SATURDAY, *was*
awarded the 1997 Newbery Medal. Ms. Konigsburg and
her husband live on the beach near Jacksonville, Florida.
Their children are grown and they have five grandchildren.

BOOK (SIC) REMEMBERED

This column is usually entitled "Books Remembered," but I have retitled it as you
see it above. I added the [sic] to show that I know how to take responsibility.
Although I may mention others in passing, I want to talk about one book remem-
bered thrice. That book is CHARLOTTE'S WEB by E.B. White.

REMEMBERED ONCE

When I was eleven and a half years old, my mother had this baby that she
named Sherry and that I thought she should be embarrassed to talk about

having at her age which was thirty-four. I never expected to like this baby of my mother's but there was nothing she could do but bring it home from the hospital once she had had it.

I had not been permitted inside the hospital at all. No one under fourteen was allowed inside. My sister Harriett was fifteen, and she got to go in and see it every time my father did which was every day except the day when they went to fetch it, and I had to wait at home.

They kept women in the hospital for a long, long post-partum back then, so it was already two weeks old when my mother stepped out of the family Plymouth and opened the receiving blanket for me to get my first look at it.

I looked. And I fell in love. Immediately and completely.

When Sherry was four, my mother went to work, and Harriett got married, so a great deal of child care fell to me. Among the things I did to entertain my little sister was to read to her. I read her things that I remembered liking. She liked the sound of my voice, and—truth be told—so did I. I enjoyed reading with expression, something that I had been taught to do in grade school and something for which I had had few requests since. I read her BEAUTY AND THE BEAST and found it sexy, and HEIDI and found it syrupy, and THE LITTLE PRINCESS and found it unlikely but cried anyway. For if there is one quality that makes children's books worth remembering, it is that a person's pleasure in them is enhanced by sharing, and no small part of this sharingness is their read-aloudedness.

By the time I left home to go to college, Sherry was in elementary school. A friend handed me a copy of CHARLOTTE'S WEB, and I found something there that I could not remember finding in a children's book before. That something is courtesy. Mr. White is courteous to Fern and Templeton and Wilbur, but most of all, Mr. White is courteous to the reader.

Because I then thought that a grown-up needed a child as reason to buy a children's book, I bought a copy of CHARLOTTE'S WEB and gave it to Sherry to read to herself.

Mr. White's book made me realize that behind a good children's book there is an author, and a good children's book author is courteous.

There is now a five year delay before the second coming of CHARLOTTE'S WEB.

REMEMBERED TWICE

I had decided that for each of my son Paul's birthdays, I would give him a book plus something else. To honor this purpose I went to India Wood's Bookstore. India Wood was an eccentric: she read the books she recommended.

I proudly told her the purpose of my visit, and she went into the little section in the back where the children's books were (even then, even now) kept and brought out CHARLOTTE'S WEB.

I told her that Paul was too young, that this was his first birthday and that I wanted to get him something he could slobber over. She told me that he was not too young to be read to and that she saw nothing wrong with his slobbering over Charlotte if it were quality slobber, that she wouldn't consider letting me start my son's library with anything else and she wouldn't let me out of the store without it.

I bought it.

I reread it.

In this reading, I found something besides courtesy that Mr. White's book has: a sense of delight.

I wanted to write.

I wanted to give a sense of delight.

Paul would be in elementary school before I would write my first book. When I sent the manuscript in, I chose to send it under the name E.L. Konigsburg because if initials were good enough for E.B., they were good enough for me. And our first initial matched.

I had written nine books and had a monumental writer's block before I again encountered Charlotte.

REMEMBERED THRICE

In 1979 my daughter Laurie was working in the archives of the library at Cornell University. I visited her there. Knowing that E.B. White was an alumnus of Cornell, I suspected that his papers would have been donated to the school. When I discovered that, indeed, they had been, I requested seeing the original materials for CHARLOTTE'S WEB. They were sent up in a basket. There I found a first draft which was not like the second draft. There was a third draft, too. There may have been a fourth; I don't remember, and it doesn't matter. What mattered to me then was that White's smooth, wonderful glissando, his perfect pitch was not effortless. His papers showed that E.B. White worked long and hard to make his prose effortlessly courteous, endlessly delightful. That he worked well is evident in the fact that no one suspects that he worked long and hard.

I returned to Jacksonville with my writer's block seriously eroded.

Laurie who made possible my last encounter with CHARLOTTE'S WEB has also made possible my next, for she is the mother of my first grandchild. His name is Samuel Todd (gorgeous, yes, thank you), and he is waiting for me to remember Charlotte with him. He doesn't know yet that he is waiting, but I know that he is. Or is it I who waits to remember?

Bibliography

(All titles published by Atheneum)

JENNIFER, HECATE, MACBETH, WILLIAM McKINLEY, AND ME, ELIZABETH, ill. by the author, 1967
FROM THE MIXED-UP FILES OF MRS. BASIL E. FRANKWEILER, ill. by the author, 1967
ABOUT THE B'NAI BAGELS, ill. by the author, 1969
GEORGE, 1970
ALTOGETHER, ONE AT A TIME, ill. by Gail E. Haley, Mercer Mayer, Gary Parker, and Laurel Schindelman, 1971
A PROUD TASTE FOR SCARLET AND MINIVER, 1973
THE DRAGON IN THE GHETTO CAPER, 1974
THE SECOND MRS. GIACONDA, ill. with reproductions of the art of Leonardo Da Vinci and others, 1975
FATHER'S ARCANE DAUGHTER, 1976
THROWING SHADOWS, 1979
JOURNEY TO AN 800 NUMBER, 1982
UP FROM JERICHO TEL, 1986
SAMUEL TODD'S BOOK OF GREAT COLORS, ill. by the author, 1990
SAMUEL TODD'S BOOK OF GREAT INVENTIONS, ill. by the author, 1991
AMY ELIZABETH EXPLORES BLOOMINGDALE'S, ill. by the author, 1992
T-BACKS, T-SHIRTS, COAT, AND SUIT, 1993
TALKTALK: A CHILDREN'S BOOK AUTHOR SPEAKS TO GROWN-UPS, 1995
THE VIEW FROM SATURDAY, 1996

Katherine Paterson

Vol. 40, No. 1, August 1985-May 1986

Samantha Loomis Paterson

Born in China, Katherine Paterson holds masters
degrees from both the Presbyterian School of Christian Education
and Union Theological Seminary. She lived and worked for
four years in Japan. Two of her novels, BRIDGE TO TERABITHIA
and JACOB HAVE I LOVED, were awarded Newbery Medals.
The Patersons live in Barre, Vermont, and have
four children and two granddaughters.

$\mathscr{U}$ntil I was nearly five, I lived in Hwaian, China. Our family had no English-speaking neighbors. There was no public library and no bookstore that sold English books, so the number of books I knew was quite limited. We did have British friends, maiden lady missionaries, who came to visit us fairly frequently. Looking back I suspect it was because my parents were more fun to be with than most of the saints they might have chosen. Anyhow, these wonderful ladies brought us volumes of A.A. Milne and Kenneth Grahame and Beatrix Potter which my mother read to us over and over again, along with JO BOY, THE REAL MOTHER GOOSE, the King James Bible, and Egermeier's Bible Story book. Among our other books were fairy tales and Kipling and A CHILD'S GARDEN OF VERSES.

For years I have wished that I could share with my own children a

Christmas book that as a four year old I thought of as the most beautiful book in the world. The book was a casualty of our refugeeing, and I've never seen it since. Finding a copy was a problem since I couldn't remember the name of the book or the illustrator, but I had a vivid picture of deep blues and gold. In thinking about this article I began searching reference books for a clue to what that wonderful book might have been. It was, of course, THE CHRIST CHILD by Maude and Miska Petersham. Now, maybe, I'll be able to locate it.

I remember the Goops, little round-faced fellows who were supposed to teach us etiquette. What endeared them to me was not their didacticism, but the fact that they taught by hilarious (to a four year old) negative example. I still identify with the Goops.

The glowing exception to the trash of those years was THE SECRET GARDEN which aroused in me the same holy fear I had felt listening to my mother read Charles Kingsley's THE WATER-BABIES. I've never tried to reread THE WATER-BABIES, suspecting somehow that it won't stand up to my four year old awe of it, but I have read THE SECRET GARDEN to my own children and rejoiced that the magic still lives.

We were refugeed again at the end of 1940, and, finally, by the next fall were located in Winston-Salem, North Carolina. Here the richest reading period of my childhood began, because, although, the school playground seemed a jungle and the classroom a place of inquisition to this expatriate nine year old, the library was a sanctuary. I can only name a few of the books I met and loved during the nearly four years I spent at Wiley School, some of them are long forgotten. But I must mention the books of Kate Seredy and Robert Lawson and Holling C. Holling. This was also the period of HANS BRINKER, HEIDI, LITTLE WOMEN and its sequels, and a new "best book I ever read," THE YEARLING.

Because I was read to so much, I began reading on my own well before I started first grade. I kept this skill a secret, because the first grade teacher in Richmond, Virginia, was unhappy enough that a five year old had been placed in her class, so I stumbled through Dick and Jane with the rest of the slow readers. Fortunately, the situation in China stabilized, and we were able to return there in early spring. Only my father was allowed to go back to Hwaian, however. The other six of us lived in Shanghai at the American School where there was a library.

You would think that a child who had been read Milne and Grahame and Potter and the Bible on her mother's lap would have great taste as a reader. I'm sorry to report that this was not the case. My Shanghai period is noted for the trash I read—THE BOBBSEY TWINS, THE LITTLE COLONEL, THE FIVE LITTLE PEPPERS, all waste, though hardly toxic, with the possible exception of Elsie Dinsmore, whose humorless moralisms proved nearly fatal to my tender spiritual development.

There were books I rejected, as well. I was terrified early on by an illustration for THE LEGEND OF SLEEPY HOLLOW, which meant that it was years before I read the story. The text of ALICE'S ADVENTURES IN WONDERLAND gave me a similar fright, and I have to confess to never enjoying the book except for some of the nonsense verses in it. Maybe, now that I'm past fifty, I should give it another try. I didn't much like DR. DOLITTLE, it seemed rather silly to me, and although at seven and eight I had devoured the Bobbsey Twins, I read one Nancy Drew mystery and gave up on that cool young sleuth. Hitty seemed much more real.

I lived long before the dawning of Young Adult Books, so my high school reading was a mishmash of old and contemporary fiction. As you can see, I never was much for non-fiction. I read the Bible, but until my college years, I always liked the stories best. My mother belonged to the Book-of-the-Month Club for a few years, and while the mothers of my friends were censoring their reading, my mother was handing me the latest bestseller, often because she had failed to return the stop card, and asking me to read the book to see if it were worth her time. As a young adolescent, I loved THE SCARLET PIMPERNEL, and years later I understood exactly what my daughter meant when she complained quietly that JACOB HAVE I LOVED wasn't quite romantic enough for her tastes. It probably wouldn't have been romantic enough for my tastes back then, either.

In my own defense, I must add that this was the age of Dickens for me. Ah, well, he is a romantic, isn't he? JANE EYRE also fed my romantic hungers but WUTHERING HEIGHTS convinced me for a while that there was no God. I'm not sure why it had this effect, but an adult friend, seeing my distress without knowing its exact nature, introduced me to the works of C.S. Lewis at just this time. It was through Lewis that I found my way to George Macdonald and eventually to Charles Williams, so I suppose I'm obliged to Emily Bronte for a great deal in a backwards sort of way.

But the book that marked the end of my youth and the beginning of my adulthood was Alan Paton's CRY THE BELOVED COUNTRY, which I read at sixteen. I recall this book when I am taken to task for failing to write "uplifting" books. This book didn't uplift me, it devastated me—not the kind of devastation that I experienced in reading WUTHERING HEIGHTS, but the kind the prophet Jeremiah speaks of when he says that his task is "...to destroy, and to throw down, to build, and to plant." That is what a great book can do for its reader. The books I have read have taught me this. So how can I presume to be a writer? That remains a mystery of grace.

Bibliography

THE SIGN OF THE CHRYSANTHEMUM, ill. by Peter Landa, Crowell, 1973
OF NIGHTINGALES THAT WEEP, ill. by Haru Wells, Crowell, 1974
THE MASTER PUPPETEER, ill. by Haru Wells, Crowell, 1976
BRIDGE TO TERABITHIA, ill. by Donna Diamond, Crowell, 1977

THE GREAT GILLY HOPKINS, Crowell, 1978
ANGELS AND OTHER STRANGERS: FAMILY CHRISTMAS STORIES, Crowell, 1979
JACOB HAVE I LOVED, Crowell, 1980
(as translator) THE CRANE WIFE, by Sumiko Yagawa, ill. by Suekichi Aabe, Morrow, 1981
REBELS OF THE HEAVENLY KINGDOM, Lodestar, 1983
COME SING, JIMMY JO, Lodestar, 1985
CONSIDER THE LILIES: PLANTS OF THE BIBLE, with John Paterson, ill. by Anne Ophelia Dowden, Crowell, 1986
(as translator) THE TONGUE-CUT SPARROW by Momoko Ishii, ill. by Suekichi Akaba, Lodestar, 1987
PARK'S QUEST, Lodestar, 1988
THE TALE OF THE MANDARIN DUCKS, ill. by Leo and Diane Dillon, Lodestar, 1990
LYDDIE, Lodestar, 1991
THE SMALLEST COW IN THE WORLD, ill. by Jane Clark Brown, HarperCollins, 1991
THE KING'S EQUAL, ill. by Vladimir Vagin, HarperCollins, 1992
WHO AM I?, ill. by Stephanie Milanowski, Eerdmans, 1992
FLIP-FLOP GIRL, Lodestar, 1994
A MIDNIGHT CLEAR: TWELVE FAMILY STORIES FOR THE CHRISTMAS SEASON, Lodestar, 1995
A SENSE OF WONDER: ON READING AND WRITING BOOKS FOR CHILDREN, Lodestar, 1995
THE ANGEL AND THE DONKEY, Clarion, 1996
JIP: HIS STORY, Lodestar, 1996

Robert Cormier

Vol. 40, No. 2, June-December 1986

Beth Bergman

*A former journalist, Robert Cormier received
the Margaret A. Edwards award for a living writer whose
"books have been accepted by young people as an authentic voice
that continues to illuminate their experiences and emotions."
He and his wife, Connie, live in Leominster, Massachusetts, less than
three miles from the house in which he was born.*

I'm almost afraid to confess to the trash I read as a boy growing up on French Hill in Leominster, Massachusetts. I was a student at St. Cecelia's Parochial School and can't truly remember a book that was introduced to me in the classroom although I fell in love with words as early as the second or third grade, and Sister Catherine, my teacher in the sixth and seventh grades, had a profound influence on my future as a writer. This influence did not derive from the books she introduced me to, however. On Friday afternoons, she read to the class the continuing adventures of Tom Playfair from a magazine whose title I've forgotten. Tom Playfair seemed like a pale character to me—as drab as his name—although certainly more interesting than arithmetic.

The comic books of the 1930s provided my first great reading, although they were neither comic, nor books. I encountered Superman in the pages of Action Comics and thrilled to this creature from the planet Krypton who leaped tall buildings at a single bound. Those were the early days of Batman and the Green Hornet and the Submariner. I also discovered magazines. First the pulps, like *Wings* and *The Shadow* magazine and *Argosy*. Later came the stories in *Colliers, The Saturday Evening Post* (to which I sold subscriptions) and *Liberty*. *Liberty* was notable for including the time it would take to read each story, as in: "Reading Time, 5 minutes, 32 seconds." I always tried to beat that time.

Such was my reading in those elementary years.

But there's a paradox here.

From the very beginning, I loved words, I loved the sound of words, the taste of them, the way vowels and consonants came together in such splendid logic, the magic an adjective conferred on a noun. I also loved poetry, throbbed to the rhymes and rhythms of poems: story poems ("And the highwayman came riding, up to the old inn-door"); poems that leaped with sound and color ("to the tintinnabulation that so musically wells/From the bells, bells, bells, bells"); sonnets that echoed my dim longings for love and romance ("How do I love thee? Let me count the ways."); or caught the drama of doomed youth ("I have a rendezvous with Death/At some disputed barricade").

I came late to books. Perhaps I loved movies too much. The Children's Room of the Public Library was never a favorite place of mine. I never joined those Vacation Reading Clubs during which Miss Spaulding issued tiny paper airplanes for every book that was read and later suspended the planes from the ceiling. I searched in vain for books that would satisfy a yearning in me that I could not identify. I found Booth Tarkington's Penrod series and followed with mild interest Penrod's adventures with his friend, Sam. I certainly must have run across TREASURE ISLAND there and perhaps DAVID COPPERFIELD although I recall him more vividly as Freddie Bartholomew in the movie. I never found what I was looking for in that children's section because, I see now, I didn't know what I was looking for.

And then a marvelous thing happened.

My Aunt Victorine, who was also my godmother, presented me with THE ADVENTURES OF TOM SAWYER on my twelfth birthday. This was the first real book I ever owned—school books didn't count—with my name inscribed on the flyleaf. This was the book that changed my ideas about reading and writing—and thus changed my life forever.

Tom Sawyer did for me what Penrod and Sam could not do (which shows the difference between the genius of Mark Twain and the mere craftsmanship of Tarkington). I laughed and cried with Tom, dreamed and schemed with him. More than that, this novel pointed out the drama possible in the life of an ordinary boy and thus the potential drama in my own life. I looked at French Hill as if for the first time and saw its mysteries and its beauties and the drama that can be found in ordinariness. Mark Twain gave me what I have always thought of as my "third eye," a secret eye that operates to this day, that allows me to see objectively the events of my life—and other lives that touch mine—as the stuff of drama.

The year I turned thirteen I walked into the Leominster Public Library and saw on a shelf marked *New Fiction* a book titled THE WEB AND THE ROCK. I can't say what drew me to this book, I only know that I scanned the jacket copy, carried it to a quiet corner of the library, and read until the library closed hours later. My senses reeled at this story of a young man's search for love and fame and fortune, the tale of a small-town youth—my God, like myself—awkward and lost and alone in the immensity of this world. I found in Wolfe the poetry that was missing in Mark Twain, the tumultuous language that shook my senses, the theme that excited my soul.

I knew when I finished that novel the inevitable course my life would take. I would be a writer. No other life would be possible for me.

Somehow I convinced Miss Wheeler, that most gentle of chief librarians, to issue me an adult card. I soon discovered the simple, aching prose of THE SUN ALSO RISES and A FAREWELL TO ARMS. I found Saroyan's THE DARING YOUNG MAN ON THE FLYING TRAPEZE and MY NAME IS ARAM, and marveled at words that were like newly-minted coins bouncing on the page.

Wolfe had dazzled me with his mountain torrent of prose but had also discouraged me. How could I ever write like that? Hemingway and Saroyan showed me the beauty of simplicity—prose that could also run clean and pure like a meadow's brook.

These were the books that sent me to the kitchen table where I first tried to capture on paper the sights and sounds, the joys and heartbreaks, of my life and my world.

From that time on, I have never stopped writing.

Or reading.

Or re-reading these heroes of mine whose brightness for me has never dimmed.

Bibliography

NOW AND AT THE HOUR, Coward McCann, 1960
A LITTLE RAW ON MONDAY MORNINGS, Sheed and Ward, 1963
TAKE ME WHERE THE GOOD TIMES ARE, Macmillan, 1965
THE CHOCOLATE WAR, Pantheon, 1974
I AM THE CHEESE, Pantheon, 1977
AFTER THE FIRST DEATH, Pantheon, 1979
EIGHT PLUS ONE, Pantheon, 1980
THE BUMBLEBEE FLIES ANYWAY, Pantheon, 1983
BEYOND THE CHOCOLATE WAR, 1985
FADE, Delacorte, 1988
OTHER BELLS FOR US TO RING, ill. by Deborah Kogan Ray, Delacorte, 1990
I HAVE WORDS TO SPEND: REFLECTIONS OF A SMALL TOWN EDITOR, Delacorte, 1991
WE ALL FALL DOWN, Delacorte, 1991

TUNES FOR BEARS TO DANCE TO, Delacorte, 1992
IN THE MIDDLE OF THE NIGHT, Delacorte, 1995
TENDERNESS, Delacorte, 1997

Eleanor Cameron

Vol. 41, No. 1, January-August 1987

Eleanor Cameron with her father

*On writing for children, Eleanor Cameron said,
"what the children's writer has to say, the stories he has to tell,
come forth most naturally and fully and freely when related to
the memories and emotions of childhood." A recipient of the National
Book Award for* THE COURT OF THE STONE CHILDREN,
Ms. Cameron lived in California until her death in 1996.

When I was asked to contribute to "Books Remembered" what came to mind immediately, without a moment's thinking, were books in three categories that have had a lifelong influence. And this instantaneous knowledge showed me patterns so neat that I distrusted them. But on reflection I couldn't distrust, because there it all was. There it all *is*.

First of all there was the Arthurian legend. I've written elsewhere how moved I was as a child of eight or nine by Arthur's life and death, a life and death that haunted me forever and that has just compelled me to buy Norma Lorre Goodrich's superb KING ARTHUR which puts him in reality up in Scotland (my husband would have been pleased!). You see, I've always wanted him to be real, as have many thousands of people. I wrote on that other occasion that Arthur's death meant the passing of goodness and courage and idealism, the breaking up of the Round Table, the scattering of the great knights; all of that gone, perhaps forever, and that I remember the unutterable poignancy I felt—sadness mixed with longing—yet a sense of exaltation, of having touched something very fine and powerful and strength-giving. For me, as a child, Arthur's story was equal to the adult experience of Greek or Shakespearean tragedy. And the idealism and the ethical principles, which were there in the philosophy that compelled Arthur to gather the Knights of the Round Table, seem to have stayed with me throughout my life.

The next influence was fairy tales. I consumed fairy tales, English, Chinese, Japanese, all I could come by in that low-ceilinged, paneled, possibly underlit room in the old Carnegie Public Library on Shattuck Avenue in Berkeley, California. I loved that room with its windows, when sunlit, turned green-gold by the light filtered through bushes and hanging boughs, and the big grandfather clock ticking comfortably, I always thought, while I sat there at one of the low tables lost in the happiness of reading.

And the love of fantasy never left me, so that, combined with the books of the astronomer Sir James Jeans that I began reading when I was seventeen, I could write a series of space fantasies for my son David many years later. Jean's descriptions of the universe and its workings I only a quarter understood, but they brought me back to his pages all through my late teens, filling me with awe and a profound respect for creation.

Now, of those fairy tales, I was apparently drawn more strongly than I then realized by the Japanese, or was more deeply impressed by them. For it was those tales that must have taken me, one afternoon after another, into the little Japanese shop on University Avenue to linger there for an hour or more, minutely examining all the small magical things that Japanese fingers had made and that are evoked in the fairy tales. Later my parents opened an import shop and gathered pieces of Japanese art for it, some of which I've inherited. But if I didn't find satisfaction in the sight of them, they'd have found no lasting place in my home. As it is, I'm surrounded by Japanese prints, small figures, wall screens and other artifacts. They delight me, and whenever I go into an art museum in a city never visited before, I make off at once for the Japanese section, where I feel that same connection the Impressionists must have felt and that they revealed through technique and style in many of their paintings and prints.

The final influence of books remembered came from the animal stories of Rudyard Kipling and the Limberlost novels of Gene Stratton-Porter. Still, after all these years, when I say over the names in THE JUNGLE BOOKS, something eerie happens—I get a *grue* (Scottish for a feathery chill) around the back of my neck and down my arms. *Bagheera,* I whisper, *Shere Khan, Mowgli, Rikki-tikki-tavi, Darzee, the Bandar-log, Baloo, Tabaqui, Kaa, the Seeonee wolf-pack, Akela, Mang the Bat, Kala Nag, Toomai of the Elephants,* and the whole world of Kipling's jungle rises up in my mind. The years fall away and there's no distance at all between the time I was ten and now. For how the man could write! And it was then I was realizing for the first time, without knowing it, that the great writer intuits names for his creatures—be they animal, bird, or human—that are deeply and beautifully *right,* that will live with us forever after along with the creatures named.

Kipling's works have lived as Gene Stratton-Porter's have not. It is true that in our small local library A GIRL OF THE LIMBERLOST is still there, the original copy I'm sure, battered and stained and smelly, but Kipling's books take up a whole shelf in many of their editions, old and new. And yet, during her lifetime, Stratton-Porter's books were translated into seven languages and during the last seventeen years of her life sold 1700 copies a day.

She was one of our first genuine conservationists, and her attachment to the swamp she lovingly called the Limberlost compelled her to risk her own safety photographing wildlife no matter what difficulties she had to undergo to get the shots she wanted. Her descriptions must have brought place vividly before this child's eyes, because the lasting result has caused in me a fierce resentment when I read about the spoliation of our wilderness areas and national parks, or any irreplaceable habitat like the South American rain forests and Alaska and the Arctic, which are being littered with the ugly remains of our search for oil.

But I'm astonished now when I read for the first time since childhood such passages in A GIRL OF THE LIMBERLOST as, "Elnora, you are the veriest Queen of Love this afternoon. From the tips of your toes to your shining crown, I worship you." My word! I remember nothing of this, so that clearly it was my devotion to the Limberlost that stayed with me, reinforced by blissful vacations in Yosemite.

My husband would tease me about all "the vanishing wildlife" mail that comes to our house, mail concerned with everything from save-the-tule elk and save-the-redwoods, to save-the-whales and save the parks and the mountain lions and the sea otters. Perhaps it all harks back in some respect to my wholehearted response when I was ten and eleven to Gene Stratton-Porter's intensely felt sense of place.

Bibliography

THE WONDERFUL FLIGHT TO THE MUSHROOM PLANET, ill. by Robert Henneberger, Little, Brown, 1954
STOWAWAY TO THE MUSHROOM PLANET, ill. by Robert Henneberger, Little, Brown, 1956
MR. BASS'S PLANETOID, ill. by Louis Darling, Little, Brown, 1958
THE TERRIBLE CHURNADRYNE, ill. by Beth and Joe Krush, Little, Brown, 1959
A MYSTERY FOR MR. BASS, ill. by Leonard Shortall, Little, Brown, 1960
THE MYSTERIOUS CHRISTMAS SHELL, ill. by Beth and Joe Krush, Little, Brown, 1961
THE BEAST WITH THE MAGICAL HORN, ill. by Beth and Joe Krush, Little, Brown, 1963
A SPELL IS CAST, ill. by Beth and Joe Krush, Little, Brown, 1964
TIME AND MR. BASS, ill. by Fred Meise, Little, Brown, 1967

THE GREEN AND BURNING TREE: ON THE WRITING AND ENJOYMENT OF
CHILDREN'S BOOKS, Little, Brown, 1969
A ROOM MADE OF WINDOWS, ill. by Trina Schart Hyman, Little, Brown, 1971
THE COURT OF THE STONE CHILDREN, Dutton, 1973
TO THE GREEN MOUNTAINS, Dutton, 1975
JULIA AND THE HAND OF GOD, ill. by Gail Owens, Dutton, 1977
BEYOND SILENCE, Dutton, 1980
THAT JULIA REDFERN, ill. by Gail Owens, Dutton, 1982
JULIA'S MAGIC, ill. by Gail Owens, Dutton, 1984
THE PRIVATE WORLDS OF JULIA REDFERN, Dutton, 1988
THE SEED AND THE VISION: ON THE WRITING AND CRITICISM OF CHILDREN'S
BOOKS, Dutton, 1992

Laurence Yep

Vol. 41, No. 2, September 1987-April 1988

Laurence Yep with his father

K. Yep

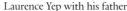

Laurence Yep has written many prize-winning
children's books, including two Newbery Honor titles and an
International Reading Association Children's Book Award winner.
His dramatic adaptation of DRAGONWINGS *was produced by the*
Kennedy Center in Washington, D.C., and by Lincoln Center
in New York City. He has taught at the University of California
at Berkeley and has won a National Endowment for the Arts fellowship.
Mr. Yep lives in Pacific Grove, California.

$\mathcal{I}$ have to confess that I did not read ALICE IN WONDERLAND and the other classics of children's literature until I was an adult.

Despite that lapse, my imagination was well-fed. As far back as I can remember, my parents always read to me—true, they were mostly comic books; but even in my earliest years I thought reading was a great pleasure. In fact, one of their major punishments was not to read to me.

Nor were comic books a total waste of time. My first real "vocabulary word" was "obnoxious"—a word I learned in LITTLE LULU. I remember actually checking it in the dictionary. And I still retain a fondness for Pogo comics where long stories were told with a wild verbal humor. And when I was ready, books were there.

But then they had to be a certain type of book. I grew up in a largely black neighborhood in San Francisco and got on the bus to go to a Catholic school in Chinatown where my brother and some of my cousins had gone. But we did not speak Chinese at home. As a result, sometimes I felt like an outsider in Chinatown. And in my own neighborhood, I was one of the few non-blacks.

As a result, the librarian could never get me interested in Homer Price and his doughnut machines. Books about children who lived in suburban houses where every child had a bike and left their front doors unlocked seemed unrealistic and even crazy.

But the Oz books opened an entirely new world for me—the Chinese caricatures in THE SCARECROW OF OZ notwithstanding. I had finally found stories that were true to my own emotional reality. In those wonderful books, children were taken out of our world and brought to Oz where they had to learn new customs and adapt to new people. So—more than HOMER PRICE—the Oz books talked about adapting, and that was something that I did every day I got on and off that bus.

Of course, I soon exhausted the Oz books, but I was now hooked. I went on to other fantasy series though FREDDY THE PIG stands out the most in my memory. I still retain a deep fondness for the slightly pompous but good-hearted writer of doggerel. (For years afterwards I could not eat tongue because it reminded me of Mrs. Wiggins.)

I soon extended my reading from fantasy to science fiction which has many of the same survival strategies. Despite the poor literary quality of the TOM CORBETT, SPACE CADET books, they will always retain a special hold on my imagination.

I suffered from asthma as a child and there were numerous nights when each breath was a struggle. Reading helped me forget myself and my condition. Often, as I sat propped up on pillows, I would drift off into a kind of half-sleep where I was one of the characters in the story.

However, one Chinatown friend thought I was weak-minded for liking science fiction. Two decades later, that same friend confessed to me that his own son liked my science fiction and fantasy books—a confession which left me both elated and embarrassed at the same time.

Despite that peer pressure, I would walk along the young adult shelves and, like my friend Elizabeth Lynn, take out any one with a rocket logo on the spine. Two special favorites were Robert Heinlein's fast-talking, funny narrators and the sad, mysterious, decaying worlds of Andre Norton.

However, this once raised unforeseen complications when it came time to check out Andre Norton's GALACTIC DERELICT. The librarian at the desk was the "Answer Man" on a radio station. Listeners would send in questions and he would provide answers on the radio. When I presented the book to him, he began to quiz me about the title. I knew what the words meant, but I was tongue-tied in front of this mini-celebrity. It wasn't until a long line had been built up behind me that he would finally stamp my card and let me go. (And I had my mother return the book.)

But soon the library wasn't the only place I went to read. I also went to a small bookstore south of Chinatown that was owned by a retired sailor. Prospective customers had to climb over his smelly old dog, Windy, who liked to lie in the sunny doorway.

It was there that I bought what felt like a real book, THE MUSEUM OF ANTIQUITIES, which had imitation leather binding and gilt letters. It had been bound upside down and the cover was torn off from the pages; but it had dozens of engraved plates, including pictures of Schliemann's discoveries at Troy. I was still impressed enough to pay fifty cents for it.

I discovered that there was a world of the past as well as a world of the future. There were quite literally worlds within worlds. And I learned that instead of walking on Mars and speaking to Martians, I could step into Roman Britain and speak to Romans. I quickly ran through the Rosemary Sutcliffs and even the wheezy boys' series written by Joseph Altsheler.

By then, Chinatown wasn't big enough for my tastes; and I wound up having to go to the main library to salve my curiosity. There were stacks and stacks of history books to be explored. (There were also flashers but avoiding them was part of the challenge of the library—like using the Dewey Decimal system.)

Though it started with something as simple as comic books, I had discovered the secret pleasure of reading—of projecting myself in my imagination through time as well as space. As a result, facts and statistics became more than dry, dusty relics. I soon discovered that they were like pieces of a hologram. Cut a hologram in half and both halves will still contain the whole. A bit of trivia about an obscure Chinese-American inventor could produce the building blocks for a world that had long since vanished.

Bibliography

SWEETWATER, ill. by Julia Noonan, Harper, 1973
DRAGONWINGS, Harper, 1975
CHILD OF THE OWL, Harper, 1977
SEADEMONS, Harper, 1977
SEA GLASS, Harper, 1979
THE MARK TWAIN MURDERS, Four Winds, 1982
KIND HEARTS AND GENTLE MONSTERS, Harper, 1982
LIAR, LIAR, Morrow, 1983
DRAGON OF THE LOST SEA, Harper, 1983
THE SERPENT'S CHILDREN, Harper, 1984
THE TOM SAWYER FIRES, Morrow, 1984
DRAGON STEEL, Harper & Row, 1985
MOUNTAIN LIGHT, Harper & Row, 1985
SHADOW LORD, Pocket, 1985
MONSTER MAKERS, INC., Arbor House, 1986
CURSE OF THE SQUIRREL, ill. by Dirk Zimmer, Random House, 1987
THE RAINBOW PEOPLE, ill. by David Wiesner, Harper, 1989
"Pay the Chinaman" in BETWEEN WORLDS, edited by M. Berson, New York: Theater Communications Group, 1990

DRAGON CAULDRON, Harper & Row, 1991
TONGUES OF JADE, ill. by David Wiesner, Harper, 1991
THE LOST GARDEN, Messner, 1991
THE STAR FISHER, Morrow, 1991
DRAGON WAR, HarperCollins, 1992
AMERICAN DRAGONS, as editor, HarperCollins, 1992
THE BUTTERFLY BOY, ill. by Jeanne M. Lee, Farrar, 1993
THE SHELL WOMAN AND THE KING: A CHINESE FOLKTALE, ill. by Yang Ming-Yi, Dial, 1993
DRAGON'S GATE, HarperCollins, 1993
THE GHOST FOX, ill. by Jean & Mou-sien Tseng, Scholastic, 1993
Playscript of DRAGONWINGS, Dramatists Guild, 1993
THE MAN WHO TRICKED A GHOST, ill. by Isadore Seltzer, BridgeWater, 1994
THE TIGER WOMAN, ill. by Robert Roth, BridgeWater, 1994
THE BOY WHO SWALLOWED SNAKES, ill. by Jean & Mou-sien Tseng, Scholastic, 1994
THE JUNIOR THUNDER LORD, ill. by Robert Van Nutt, BridgeWater, 1994
HIROSHIMA, Scholastic, 1995
THE CITY OF DRAGONS, ill. by Jean & Mou-sien Tseng, Scholastic, 1995
LATER GATOR, Hyperion, 1995
THIEF OF HEARTS, HarperCollins, 1995
THE TREE OF DREAMS: TEN TALES FROM THE GARDEN OF NIGHT, ill. by Isadore Seltzer, Troll, 1995
RIBBONS, Putnam, 1996
THE MONGOLIAN SHEPHERD, ill. by Jean & Mou-sien Tseng, Scholastic, 1996
THE CASE OF THE GOBLIN PEARLS, HarperCollins, 1997
DRAGON PRINCE, ill.by Kam Mak, HarperCollins, 1997

Plays

PAY THE CHINAMAN and FAIRY BONES produced by the Asian-American Theater Company in September, 1987, and Pan-Asian Repertory in May, 1992.
DRAGONWINGS produced by Berkeley Repertory Theatre, September-December, 1991; Lincoln Center and Kennedy Center, Fall 1992. Remounted at Berkeley Theatre, December 1992; Seattle Children's Theater, Spring 1993; Atlanta Alliance Theater, Fall 1993; Honolulu Theatre for Youth, Fall 1994; Syracuse Stage, Spring 1995.

Betsy Byars

Vol. 41, No. 3, May-December 1988

Susan Valdina

*Betsy Byars credits her own teenagers with teaching her
that she must not write down to her readers; she must write up to them.
A recipient of the Newbery Medal for* THE SUMMER OF THE
SWANS, *her books are frequent winners of children's choice awards.
Born and raised in the south, Ms. Byars now lives with her
husband on an airstrip in Clemson, South Carolina.*

THE LURE OF THE CHAPTER

*A*t the age of four, I became a reading snob. There were no pre-schools
or kindergartens back then, but my older sister and I played 'School' on
rainy days, and she had taught me to read. I was proud of my skill, loved
books and read aloud to anyone who would listen. My one aversion was to
books of fairy tales because the family one always fell open, as if by bad
magic, to the picture of One Eye, Two Eyes and Three Eyes. Years before,
someone had tried mercifully to remove the third eye from the sister's fore-
head with an eraser, but you could still see it if you knew what to look for.

Then came the discovery that turned me from a loving reader into an
instant and terrible snob. My sister's books, it turned out, had something
mine did not—she herself pointed out the difference. Her books had chap-

ters. Chapters! Suddenly my beloved books became childish toys. "But I thought you loved THE TALE OF CORALLY CROTHERS," my mother would say, "it's your favorite." "It doesn't have chapters," I would answer with real regret.

I recall the excitement I felt as I worked my way through my first chapter book at last! It was Harry Thurston Peck's THE ADVENTURES OF MABEL, and it proved the vast superiority of books with chapters by being the best book in the entire world. It seemed to have been written expressly for me. It catered to my personal appetites—love of nature, desire for imaginative adventure and need for a world that lovingly revolved around its core—myself. For the first time I knew the thrill of identification. I became Mabel. Rex was my horse. The frogs, gallantly lined up on the unsafe bridge, risking cruel death beneath Rex's hooves, were there to warn me of danger. I remember I worked out on the piano the seven notes of the Lizard's Call which, as soon as I learned to whistle, would enable me to communicate with wild animals.

Now that I had experienced the unique power of chapter books, I accepted chapters as the criteria of literary excellence and began to devour trash. I read every popular series there was—Uncle Wiggly, the Bobbsey twins, Nancy Drew. I loved the books about Maida, whose millionaire father gave her islands and circuses to make up for her twisted leg. I read the books Leo Edwards wrote for boys and sent off two three-cent stamps to join his literary club—"The Secret and Mysterious Order of the Freckled Goldfish."

I preferred series books because the identification was built-in, triggered by the familiar look of the jacket before the first sentence had been read. My bond with even the most cardboard of main characters was so intense, their perils and pleasures so much my own, that my mother sometimes interrupted to ask me not to make so many faces when I read.

This marathon of series reading ended in the middle of third grade. We had been living in a cotton mill community where my sister and I attended a mill school. We now moved into the city of Charlotte, and I went to a public library for the first time in my life. My sister and I rode the bus downtown together, and I was excited.

Up until this moment, I had never been out of the Carolinas—except the one time my father drove us into the tip of Georgia so we would claim a third state—and the most impressive thing I had seen was the Atlantic Ocean. The grandeur of the ocean was nothing compared to the Charlotte Public Library where the dark stacks of books went all the way up into the stratosphere. My sister, two years older and a woman of the world, said, "I'll show you where the good books are." I followed her gratefully to a section of romances where she chose a book by Margaret Pedler, and I did too. She got THE FLAME OF PASSION. I got THE VISION OF DESIRE. Margaret Pedler books were not easy reads for a third grader. They were four hundred pages long. In the first five pages, a spunky

English girl and a gray-eyed Englishman of noble birth fell hopelessly in love, and then for the next three hundred and ninety-four pages they were kept apart. · In the end, the various mix-ups would be quickly solved, and the united couple would do something like 'Go forth together into the future, unafraid,' which was exactly what I myself intended to do as soon as my parents would let me.

The Margaret Pedlers were not a series, but the spunky English girls all had a lot in common, and I slipped easily into jodhpurs and simple tweed jackets. Certainly I was firmly in place by page two or three, anticipating the electric moment when the noble gray eyes would look piercingly into mine. I checked out my favorites again and again. My signature appeared sometimes ten times on one card, with the monotony of 'Betsy Cromer' broken occasionally by the infrequent name of another reader.

Later that year, I ventured over to the next section and discovered new satisfactions in a life on the plains. My favorite western role, hands down, was that of Bess the rustler girl in RIDERS OF THE PURPLE SAGE. My name was on that card a lot too, and I can still recall vivid details of the cave that I shared platonically with Venters. After that, I pretty much worked my way through the library, reading everything that caught my attention, establishing a life-long reading pattern that consisted almost entirely of what I thought of as real life fiction. I did not have a flicker of interest in the authors of the books I read or in becoming one myself.

Years passed, and I found myself once again in the dark, now-familiar stacks as part of a High School tour on library use. I was not paying attention—I already knew where the good books were—when the librarian startled me by saying, "Now, I'll show you the children's collection." The what?

She led us down a long hall to a room I had not known existed—a room as secret as those Nancy Drew and I had searched for long ago. Unaccustomed to such brightness, I stood blinking in the book-lined room. Surely some librarian must have attempted to bring me here, I thought. After all, I had not been really mature enough in appearance to be checking out THE VISION OF DESIRE. My snapshots of that year resemble an underfed Campbell Soup kid.

Yet even as I stood there, an uninvited guest at a party long over, I faced the unbecoming truth. If a dedicated librarian had managed to dislodge me from the dark stacks and lead me to this room with all its cheerful splendors, I would have been far too much of a snob to have enjoyed it.

Bibliography

CLEMENTINE, ill. by Charles Wilton, Houghton, 1962
THE DANCING CAMEL, ill. by Harold Berson, Viking, 1965
RAMA, THE GYPSY CAT, ill. by Peggy Bacon, Viking, 1966
THE GROOBER, ill. by the author, Harper, 1967
THE MIDNIGHT FOX, ill. by Ann Grifalconi, Viking, 1968

TROUBLE RIVER, ill. by Rocco Negri, Viking, 1969
THE SUMMER OF THE SWANS, ill. by Ted CoConis, Viking, 1970
GO AND HUSH THE BABY, ill. by Emily Arnold McCully,Viking, 1971
THE HOUSE OF WINGS, ill. by Daniel Schwartz, Viking, 1972
THE WINGED COLT OF CASA MIA, ill. by Richard Cuffari, Viking, 1973
THE 18TH EMERGENCY, ill. by Robert Grossman, Viking, 1973
AFTER THE GOAT MAN, ill. by Ronald Himler, Viking, 1974
THE LACE SNAIL, ill. by the author, Viking, 1975
THE TV KID, ill. by Richard Cuffari, Viking, 1976
THE PINBALLS, Harper, 1977
THE CARTOONIST, ill. by Richard Cuffari, Viking, 1978
GOODBYE, CHICKEN LITTLE, Harper, 1979
THE NIGHT SWIMMERS, ill. by Troy Howell, Delacorte, 1980
THE CYBIL WAR, ill. by Gail Owens, Viking, 1981
THE ANIMAL, THE VEGETABLE AND JOHN D. JONES, ill. by Ruth Sanderson,
Delacorte, 1982
THE TWO-THOUSAND-POUND GOLDFISH, Harper, 1982
THE GLORY GIRL, Viking, 1983
THE COMPUTER NUT, Viking, 1984
CRACKER JACKSON, Viking, 1985
THE GOLLY SISTERS GO WEST, ill. by Sue Truesdell, Harper, 1986
THE NOT-JUST-ANYBODY FAMILY, ill. by Jacqueline Rogers, Delacorte, 1986
THE BLOSSOMS MEET THE VULTURE LADY, ill. by Jacqueline Rogers
Delacorte, 1986
THE BLOSSOMS AND THE GREEN PHANTOM, ill. by Jacqueline Rogers,
Delacorte, 1987
A BLOSSOM PROMISE, ill. by Jacqueline Rogers, Delacorte, 1987
THE BURNING QUESTIONS OF BINGO BROWN, Viking, 1988
BEANS ON THE ROOF, ill. by Melodye Rosales, Delacorte, 1988
BINGO BROWN AND THE LANGUAGE OF LOVE, Viking, 1989
HOORAY FOR THE GOLLY SISTERS, ill. by Sue Truesdell,
HarperCollins, 1990
BINGO BROWN, GYPSY LOVER, Viking, 1990
THE SEVEN TREASURE HUNTS, ill. by Jennifer Barrett, HarperCollins, 1991
WANTED...MUD BLOSSOM, ill. by Jacqueline Rogers, Delacorte, 1991
THE MOON AND I, Silver Burdett, 1992
BINGO BROWN'S GUIDE TO ROMANCE, Viking, 1992
COAST TO COAST, Delacorte, 1992
McMUMMY, Viking, 1993
THE GOLLY SISTERS RIDE AGAIN, ill. by Sue Truesdell,
HarperCollins, 1994
THE DARK STAIRS: A HERCULEAH JONES MYSTERY, Viking, 1994
TAROT SAYS BEWARE: A HERCULEAH JONES MYSTERY, Viking, 1995
MY BROTHER ANT, ill. by Marc Simont, Viking, 1996
TORNADO, ill. by Doron Ben-Ami, HarperCollins, 1996
THE JOY BOYS, ill. by Frank Remkiewicz, Delacorte, 1996
A BEAN BIRTHDAY, ill. by Melodye Rosales, Macmillan, 1996
DEAD LETTER: A HERCULEAH JONES MYSTERY, Viking, 1996

Eve Merriam

Vol. 42, No. 1, January-June 1989

Eve Merriam and
her brother Lou

Bachrach

*Eve Merriam was one of America's most beloved and
anthologized poets as well as a writer of plays, fiction, and nonfiction.
The winner of the 1981 National Council of Teachers of English Award
for Excellence in Poetry for Children, she said, "I think one is chosen
to be a poet. You write poems because you must write them; because
you can't live your life without writing them." Ms. Merriam
lived in New York City until her death in 1992.*

Saturday was a shining silver day in our household in Philadelphia.
Starting from when I was about eight, and brother Lou was a year and a
half older, we were allotted a quarter apiece, twenty-five whole cents to
spend as we wished. The candy store next to school had its allure, of
course: strips of candy buttons, green spearmint leaves, ropes of licorice,
miniature tin cups of sickeningly sweet pink or ivory fudge along with a
tiny spoon for an elf who lived in a thimble. You could get a lot for your
quarter.

However, a quarter was also a half. Half the price of a book, a book to
buy, to take home and unwrap and keep for your own forever. If my brother and I pooled our wealth, we could have the makings of our own home
library.

60

It was hard on Saturdays to wait until afternoon when our big sister Helen would be ready to chaperone us to the bookstore. I kept transferring the heavy coin from one sweaty palm to the other, not trusting it to my pockets or knotted handkerchief. Finally, after all the hourlong minutes, we were on our way. Hurrying along Kensington Avenue where the overhead tracks of the elevated train made striped patterns on the asphalt below. We went past the bright pink neon sign for Martex towels, past the giant wooden bottle with the H advertising Harbison's Milk. My brother was as eager as I. We pulled our sister at a near trot past the ladies' clothing store, the grocery, the eyeglasses store, the pawn shop, the crockery store with chipped cup bargains overflowing onto the sidewalk. Past a scraggly field where goats still grazed, past the funeral parlor, the hardware store, the public square, and there, o splendid site, on the next corner, at last, the magical kingdom with shelves stacked from floor to ceiling with red, blue, black, brown, gold-colored bindings.

As soon as we entered, I went straight to the right shelf, for I knew exactly what I wanted. A Honey Bunch book. Any one in the series. Honey Bunch had her picture on the cover; she looked just like Shirley Temple with blonde curls, blue hair ribbon to match her blue eyes, dimples in her cheeks, her chin, and dimpled knees. What wouldn't I give to look like her! But I could clutch the book of her to my heart. As soon, that is, as my brother handed over his quarter to me. I couldn't understand why he refused to cooperate. Instead, he was opting for Tom Swift. Any one in the series. There was no winning him over to the pinafore side. If I offered my quarter towards a Tom Swift this Saturday, would he agree to buying a Honey Bunch next week? "Maybe," he grudged. Well, maybe was better than Cross my heart and hope to say Never.

Next week, alas, it was Tom Swift again. In all fairness, Lou let me borrow the books to read when he finished, and I must say I enjoyed Tom's, Ned's and Mr. Wakefield Damon's adventures with their electrical motor car, their flying machine, and Mr. Damon's Bless my shoe buttons lingo. (The Tom Swifties jokes of recent years always amuse me. "Don't give up the ship," Tom said craftily.) At least one week we did have a harmonious compromise; we bought BUNNY BROWN AND HIS SISTER SUE.

The next great purchase was NOBODY'S BOY. My feminist consciousness had not yet developed; I identified totally with Hector Malot's poor little French orphan lad. When I found NOBODY'S GIRL it seemed an inadequate whimpering sequel.

A later highlight was THE SWISS FAMILY ROBINSON: the saga of the shipwreck and the ways that family members found to survive never failed to amaze me, no matter how many times I read the book over. Most of all, I was enchanted with Mother Robinson's salvage from the devastation of the sea. Whatever anyone needed could somehow be brought to fruition with one of the mundane yet marvelous items in her pack: a nee-

dle, thread, a bit of cloth. Only years later did I realize how like Mother
Robinson my own mother was, she who made the contents of our every
day glow; pointing out the deliciousness of the crust on a loaf of bread,
savoring the pale color of butter, the skin of a dusky slippery plum, creamy
petals from the dogwood tree in our backyard, the lively slap slap of wash
on the line.

My best friends Doris and Nancy read career books. Not for me; the
books all seemed to be biographies of Florence Nightingale or Clara Barton
and nursing was not my future choice. So I read fairy tales by the score,
Grimm, Andersen, all the Andrew Lang color collections. And I also discovered the editorial page of our local newspaper, *The Bulletin*. Not that I
was precociously interested in politics, but there was a column by Tom
Daly, a practitioner of light verse and a perpetrator of dreadful puns (the
only kind there are). My brother and I recited the verses aloud, alternating
lines and cracking ourselves up.

> Ebenezer had a girl,
> Ebenezer's girl was Flo;
> Talk of tides of love, great Caesar!
> You should see them—Eb and Flo.

Another quatrain I remember, not as devastating in its nudge nudge wink
wink as the lovers, but nevertheless a gloriously disreputable retort to polite
table manners:

> I eat my peas with honey.
> I have done it all my life;
> They do taste kind of funny.
> But it keeps them on the knife.

Those light verse columns led me directly to other book treats; the 'book'
or libretto and lyrics of W.S. Gilbert in conjunction with Arthur Sullivan's
music for their famous string of operettas. By now my allowance had
swelled to fifty cents a week, so I could afford a second balcony seat for the
D'Oyly Carte productions of G. and S. that came frequently to the downtown Philadelphia theaters. My Saturday afternoons at the book store were
transformed into Saturday matinees. During the week, I was a frequent
visitor—more like a boarder—in the stacks of the school library and the
public library branch.

There was, mercifully, no Young Adult category, no separating out of
teenagers from other humans. Wherever you wanted to browse, there you
browsed. In that way I became a fan of Raphael Sabatini's Scaramouche
and of Edmond Rostand's Cyrano; of Christopher Morley's THE
HAUNTED BOOKSHOP and PARNASSUS ON WHEELS; of

Palgrave's GOLDEN TREASURY, of the three B's—Browning, Byron and Burns.

I still prefer browsing to heading directly with a certified list in hand. Serendipity is the best, and oh yes, I discovered Hugh Walpole, who coined the word. There is also the lovely idle leafing through anthologies, which is how I first came upon the "Pied Beauty" of Gerard Manley Hopkins; the reverberating shock waves of "Glory be to God for dappled things—...All things counter, original, spare, strange; Whatever is fickle, freckled (who knows how?)..." That led me to seek out a book of Hopkins' poems, another book of his letters, and his notebooks and sketches. And to his lines that I have over my desk now as I write this: the lines that I memorized unconsciously because I read them over and delightfully over:

> What would the world be, once bereft
> Of wet and of wildness? Let them be left,
> O let them be left, wildness and wet;
> Long live the weeds and the wilderness yet.

The glories of nature and the bittersweet joys of human nature, that is what books have brought into my life.

Bibliography

THE REAL BOOK ABOUT FRANKLIN D. ROOSEVELT, ill. by Bette J. Davis, Doubleday, 1952
THE REAL BOOK OF AMAZING BIRDS, ill. by Paul Wenck, Doubleday, 1952
THE VOICE OF LIBERTY: THE STORY OF EMMA LAZARUS, ill. by Charles W. Walker, Farrar, 1959
A GAGGLE OF GEESE, ill. by Paul Galdone, Knopf, 1960
MOMMIES AT WORK, ill. by Beni Montresor, Knopf, 1961; ill. by Eugenie Fernandes, Simon & Schuster, 1989
THERE IS NO RHYME FOR SILVER, ill. by Joseph Schindelman, Atheneum, 1962
FUNNY TOWN, ill. by Evaline Ness, Crowell Collier, 1963
WHAT'S IN THE MIDDLE OF A RIDDLE?, ill. by Murray Tinkelman, Collier, 1963
IT DOESN'T ALWAYS HAVE TO RHYME, ill. by Malcolm Spooner, Atheneum, 1964
WHAT CAN YOU DO WITH A POCKET?, ill. by Harriet Simon, Knopf, 1964
DO YOU WANT TO SEE SOMETHING?, ill. by Abner Graboff, Scholastic, 1965
DON'T THINK ABOUT A WHITE BEAR, ill. by Murray Tinkelman, Putnam, 1965
SMALL FRY, ill. by Garry Mackenzie, Knopf, 1965
THE STORY OF BEN FRANKLIN, ill. by Brinton Turkle, Four Winds, 1965
CATCH A LITTLE RHYME, ill. by Imero Gobbato, Atheneum, 1966
MISS TIBBETT'S TYPEWRITER, ill. by Rick Schreiter, Knopf, 1966
ANDY ALL YEAR ROUND, ill. by M. Hoff, Funk & Wagnalls, 1967
EPAMINONDAS, ill. by Trina Schart Hyman, Follett, 1968; as THAT NOODLE-HEAD EPAMINONDAS, Scholastic, 1972
INDEPENDENT VOICES, ill. by Arvis Stewart, Atheneum, 1968
THE INNER CITY MOTHER GOOSE, Simon & Schuster, 1969, 1982; ill. by David Diaz, Simon & Schuster, 1996
FINDING A POEM, ill by Seymour Chwast, Atheneum, 1970
ANIMAL TALES, as translator, by Hana Doskocilova, ed. by William H. Armstrong, ill. by Mirko Hanak, Doubleday, 1971

I AM A MAN: ODE TO MARTIN LUTHER KING, JR., ill. by Suzanne Verrier, Doubleday, 1971

PROJECT 1-2-3, ill. by Harriet Sherman, McGraw-Hill, 1971

BAM! ZAM! BOOM! A BUILDING BOOK, ill. by William Lightfoot, Walker, 1972

BOYS AND GIRLS, GIRLS AND BOYS, ill. by Harriet Sherman, Holt, 1972

MALE AND FEMALE UNDER 18: FRANK COMMENTS BY YOUNG PEOPLE ABOUT THEIR SEX ROLES TODAY, as co-editor with Nancy Larrick, Discus Books, 1973

OUT LOUD, ill. by Harriet Sherman, Atheneum, 1973

RAINBOW WRITING, Atheneum, 1976

AB TO ZOGG: A LEXICON FOR SCIENCE FICTION AND FANTASY READERS, ill. by Albert Lorenz, Atheneum, 1977

THE BIRTHDAY COW, ill. by Guy Michel, Knopf, 1978

UNHURRY HARRY, ill. by Gail Owens, Four Winds, 1978

GOOD NIGHT TO ANNIE, ill. by John Wallner, Four Winds, 1979; ill. by Carol Schwartz, Hyperion, 1992

A WORD OR TWO WITH YOU, ill. by John Nez, Atheneum, 1981

IF ONLY I COULD TELL YOU: POEMS FOR YOUNG LOVERS AND DREAMERS, ill. by Donna Diamond, Knopf, 1983

JAMBOREE: RHYMES FOR ALL TIMES, ill. by Walter Gaffney-Kessell, Dell, 1984

BLACKBERRY INK, ill. by Hans Wilhelm, Morrow, 1985

THE CHRISTMAS BOX, ill. by David Small, Morrow, 1985

THE BIRTHDAY DOOR, ill. by Peter J. Thornton, Morrow, 1986

FRESH PAINT: NEW POEMS, ill. by David Frampton, Macmillan, 1986

A SKY FULL OF POEMS, ill. by Walter Gaffney-Kessell, Dell, 1986

HALLOWEEN ABC, ill. by Lane Smith, Macmillan, 1987

YOU BE GOOD AND I'LL BE NIGHT: JUMP-ON-THE-BED-POEMS, ill. by Karen L. Schmidt, Morrow, 1988

CHORTLES: NEW AND SELECTED WORDPLAY POEMS, ill. by Sheila Hamanaka, Morrow, 1989

DADDIES AT WORK, ill. by Eugenie Fernandez, Simon & Schuster, 1989

A POEM FOR A PICKLE: FUNNYBONE VERSES, ill. by Sheila Hamanaka, Morrow, 1989

WHERE IS EVERYBODY?, ill. by Diane DeGroat, Simon & Schuster, 1989

THE WISE WOMAN AND HER SECRET, ill. by Linda Graves, Simon & Schuster, 1991

FIGHTING WORDS, ill. by David Small, Morrow, 1992

THE SINGING GREEN: NEW AND SELECTED POEMS FOR ALL SEASONS, ill. by Kathleen C. Howell, Morrow, 1992

TRAIN LEAVES THE STATION, ill. by Dale Gottlieb, Holt, 1992

SHHH!, ill. by Sheila Hamanaka, Simon & Schuster, 1993

TWELVE WAYS TO GET TO ELEVEN, ill. by Bernie Karlin, Simon & Schuster, 1993

HIGGLE WIGGLE: HAPPY RHYMES, ill. by Hans Wilhelm, Morrow, 1994

BAM BAM BAM, ill. by Dan Yaccarino, Holt, 1995

THE HOLE STORY, ill. by Ivan Chermayeff, Simon & Schuster, 1995

WHAT IN THE WORLD?, HarperCollins, 1997

Jean Fritz

Vol. 42, No. 2, July-December, 1989

Born and raised in China, Jean Fritz couldn't wait to become a "real" American. When she grew up, she immersed herself in American history, coming up with characters she wanted to figure out and remember. Her remarkable ability to bring history to life has won her high acclaim, including the Laura Ingalls Wilder Award for her "substantial and lasting contribution to literature for children." Ms. Fritz lives in Dobbs Ferry, New York.

BOOKS STILL ON MY SHELVES

I am not famous in my family for my ability to organize *things:* pots and pans, dresser drawers, closets, files, books. It's the lack of organization on my book shelves that distresses me the most. Not only are my books in disarray, they are in plain sight, begging for help. I think of the satisfaction that Alistair Cooke must take in his Americana library organized, so I've been told, like the map of America. Books on Maine are in the upper right-hand shelf next to New Hampshire and Vermont, proceeding vertically through all the states north to south, and horizontally east to west. A map won't do for my collection, but still I'd like some organization. A personal one.

Let's try this. Why not line up my children's books in the way they live in my mind? Emotionally.

1. *A Shelf of "Comfy" Books*—those lovely reassuring stories that represent the world as a manageable, domestic place where one feels cozily at home. Beatrix Potter will certainly have the honored place here with THE TALE OF TOM KITTEN coming first. Books in this category, I have found, have been "Good Books To Be Sick With." I remember the marvelously free, pampered sensation of snuggling down in a sickbed with PETER PAN, DOCTOR DOLITTLE, THE FIVE LITTLE PEPPERS, MOTHER WEST WIND, the Rosemary books, mainly because Rosemary did her reading on a window seat. (Why didn't I have a window seat? Why don't I now?) In addition, there were many British books (lost over the years), all with nice warm toy-filled nurseries and nannies serving cambric tea and toast. And of course Stevenson's A CHILD'S GARDEN OF VERSES was always on my sickbed, for who else knew "The Land of Counterpane" as well as he?

2. *Books for Crying.* After weeping over two of my favorite books, THE SECRET GARDEN and SARAH CREWE, I knew I never wanted to go to India. In China I was at least with my parents, but children of foreign parents in India were invariably sent to England and led lonely, unhappy lives. Rudyard Kipling's autobiography, SOMETHING OF MYSELF (although not a children's book), belongs next to SARAH CREWE and THE SECRET GARDEN to prove how true these books were and to show how much I have always loved Rudyard Kipling.

For some reason the sad books seem to be the most memorable. Nothing ever proved to be as reliable a tear-jerker as Eugene Field's LITTLE BOY BLUE whose "little toy soldier," still faithfully waited for his master who promised to return but died in his trundle bed. The page is still smudged with my tears yet it is Maxfield Parrish's illustrations that have saved this book from the second-hand dealer. Later of course there was LITTLE WOMEN and most devastating of all, THE MAN WITHOUT A COUNTRY. I never cried over THE LITTLE MATCH GIRL. I knew Hans Christian Andersen wanted me to cry but he wanted it too much.

3. *Spine-tingling Books.* Words alone have as much power as stories to tingle the spine and send the blood racing. It doesn't matter if I never see "the great grey greasy Limpopo River." I will always delight, O Best Beloved, in its great gray greasiness. Indeed, I think that these JUST SO STORIES of Kipling's were the natural predecessor to all the poetry on these shelves. In the British School in Hankow we had to memorize reams of poetry and for this I have always been grateful. So the presence of Tennyson and Milton and Wordsworth and Keats among my children's books is entirely legitimate. "The splendor falls on castle walls." Of course my spine tingled.

There are other kinds of spine tinglers. TREASURE ISLAND is the foremost. THE LEGEND OF SLEEPY HOLLOW was deliciously scary for me, although I realize that today a pumpkin head is nothing compared to planets on the rampage. I was supposed to be impressed by THE ADVENTURES OF PINOCCHIO but when my mother read it aloud, I could only feel guilt. There was a moral edge to her voice. Did she know I sometimes told lies?

But look at the good books left over—books that weren't around in my childhood. Please allow me just one shelf for modern books—actually, for books I wish I had written.

4. *Books I Wish I Had Written.* THE LEMMING CONDITION will be there by Alan Arkin; KNEE KNOCK RISE and TUCK EVERLAST-ING, both by Natalie Babbitt; GENTLEHANDS by M.E. Kerr; M.C. HIGGINS THE GREAT by Virginia Hamilton; HOW DOES A CZAR EAT POTATOES? by Ann Rose; THE SHRINKING OF TREEHORN by Florence Heide; THE ALFRED SUMMER by Jan Slepian. All are breath-takingly original. All have profound comments to make on the human condition.

5. *Books about Childhood.* Still, it is not only books written for children but books written about childhood that deserve a special place in my library, for after all what am I doing but running back and forth across the time zones in my life? So of course I want to explore the territory of others who make such journeys. Just to see the titles of some of their books, were they to be lined up beside each other, would make me catch my breath. SPEAK MEMORY (Vladimir Nabokov), SURPRISED BY JOY (C.S. Lewis), LOST PARADISE (Robert P. Tristram Coffin), VIVE MOI (Sean O'Faolain), AN ONLY CHILD (Frank O'Connor), GROWING PAINS (Wanda Gág), and even better—THE BOOK OF MAGGIE OWEN, a diary straight out of childhood. "I am a virgin twelve years of age," Maggie tells us. "Spinster and demoiselle and maiden mean the same thing, but not quite. I call myself a virgin and it sounds higher minded and more spiritu-al."

Best of all, however, is Dylan Thomas writing in prose—catching up pictures and feelings and places and people in deliciously long sentences with words running so unexpectedly into other words that they strike sparks. Often on a dull morning when words seem heavy, awkward things to manipulate, I will read a paragraph or two from ADVENTURES IN THE SKIN TRADE or PORTRAIT OF THE ARTIST AS A YOUNG DOG or A CHILD'S CHRISTMAS IN WALES, and the sense of magic will return and I'll be ready to write.

But as to this business of organizing, I give up. I never mentioned Alfred Noyes' trilogy in verse on the lives of scientists—THE BOOK OF EARTH, WATCHERS OF THE SKY, and the third which I have lost. Also there is Van Loon's LIVES. And these books, first met in high school, may have had the most direct influence on my own writing. But why should I make place cards for my books? Let them sit wherever they wish.

Bibliography

BUNNY HOPWELL'S FIRST SPRING, ill. by Rachel Dixon, Wonder, 1954
HELP MR. WILLY NILLY, ill. by Jean Tamburine, Treasure, 1954
FISH HEAD, ill. by Marc Simont, Coward, 1954
121 PUDDING STREET, ill. by Sofia, Coward, 1955
GROWING UP, ill. by Elizabeth Webbe, Rand McNally, 1956
THE LATE SPRING, ill. by Erik Blegvad, Coward, 1957
THE ANIMALS OF DR. SCHWEITZER, ill. by Douglas Howland, Coward, 1958
THE CABIN FACED WEST, ill. by Feodor Rojankovsky, Coward, 1958
CHAMPION DOG, PRINCE TOM, with Tom Clute, ill. by Ernest Hart, Coward, 1958
HOW TO READ A RABBIT, ill. by Leonard Shortall, Coward, 1959
BRADY, ill. by Lynd Ward, Coward, 1960
SAN FRANCISCO, ill. by Emil Weiss, Rand McNally, 1962
TAP, TAP, LION — 1, 2, 3, ill. by Leonard Shortall, Coward, 1962
I, ADAM, ill. by Peter Burchard, Coward, 1963
MAGIC TO BURN, ill. by Beth and Joe Krush, Coward, 1964
SURPRISE PARTY, ill. by George Wiggins, Initial Teaching Alphabet Publications, 1965
THE TRAIN, ill. by Jean Simpson, Grosset & Dunlap, 1965
EARLY THUNDER, ill. by Lynd Ward, Coward, 1967
GEORGE WASHINGTON'S BREAKFAST, ill. by Paul Galdone, Coward, 1969
AND THEN WHAT HAPPENED, PAUL REVERE?, ill. by Margot Tomes, Coward, 1973
WHY DON'T YOU GET A HORSE, SAM ADAMS?, ill. by Trina Schart Hyman, Coward, 1974
WHERE WAS PATRICK HENRY ON THE 29th OF MAY?, ill. by Margot Tomes, Coward, 1975
WHO'S THAT STEPPING ON PLYMOUTH ROCK?, ill. by J.B. Handelsman, Coward, 1975
WILL YOU SIGN HERE, JOHN HANCOCK?, ill. by Trina Schart Hyman, Coward, 1976
WHAT'S THE BIG IDEA, BEN FRANKLIN?, ill. by Margot Tomes, Coward, 1976
CAN'T YOU MAKE THEM BEHAVE, KING GEORGE?, ill. by Tomie dePaola, Coward, 1977
BRENDAN THE NAVIGATOR: A HISTORY MYSTERY ABOUT THE DISCOVERY OF AMERICA, ill. by Enrico Arno, Coward, 1979
STONEWALL, ill. by Stephen Gammell, Putnam, 1979
WHERE DO YOU THINK YOU'RE GOING, CHRISTOPHER COLUMBUS?, ill. by Margot Tomes, Putnam, 1980
THE MAN WHO LOVED BOOKS, ill. by Trina Schart Hyman, Putnam, 1981
TRAITOR: THE CASE OF BENEDICT ARNOLD, Putnam, 1981
THE GOOD GIANTS AND THE BAD PUKWUDGIES, ill. by Tomie dePaola, Putnam, 1982
HOMESICK: MY OWN STORY, ill. by Margot Tomes, Putnam, 1982
THE DOUBLE LIFE OF POCAHONTAS, ill. by Ed Young, Putnam, 1983
CHINA HOMECOMING, photos by Michael Fritz, Putnam, 1985
MAKE WAY FOR SAM HOUSTON, ill. by Elise Primavera, Putnam, 1986
SHH! WE'RE WRITING THE CONSTITUTION, ill. by Tomie dePaola, Putnam, 1987
CHINA'S LONG MARCH: 6,000 MILES OF DANGER, ill. by Yang Zhr Cheng, Putnam, 1988
THE GREAT LITTLE MADISON, Putnam, 1989
BULLY FOR YOU, TEDDY ROOSEVELT!, ill. by Mike Wimmer, Putnam, 1991
THE GREAT ADVENTURE OF CHRISTOPHER COLUMBUS: A POP-UP BOOK, ill. by Tomie dePaola, Putnam, 1992
GEORGE WASHINGTON'S MOTHER, ill. by Dyanne DiSalvo-Ryan, Grossett, 1992
SURPRISING MYSELF, Richard Owens, 1992
THE WORLD IN 1492, with Katherine Paterson, Patricia & Fredrick McKissack, Margaret Mahy, and Jamake Highwater, Holt, 1992
AROUND THE WORLD IN 100 YEARS: HENRY THE NAVIGATOR TO MAGELLAN, ill. by Anthony Bascon Venti, Putnam, 1993
JUST A FEW WORDS, MR. LINCOLN: THE STORY OF THE GETTYSBURG ADDRESS, ill. by Charles Robinson, Grossett, 1993
HARRIET BEECHER STOWE AND THE BEECHER PREACHERS, Putnam, 1994
YOU WANT WOMEN TO VOTE, LIZZIE STANTON?, ill. by Anne DiSalvo-Ryan, Putnam, 1995

Patricia Wrightson

Vol. 43, No. 1, January-June 1990

*Patricia Wrightson received the 1986 Hans Christian Andersen
Award for the body of her work for young readers. Four of her
books have won the Australian Book of the Year Award, including*
A LITTLE FEAR, *which also received the Boston Globe-Horn Book
Award. Ms. Wrightson lives on a narrow strip of stony ridge on the
North Coast of New South Wales, Australia, which, through her efforts,
was recently declared a national flora and fauna reserve.*

In Australia in the 1920s and 30s, libraries were hidden away in solemn
municipal buildings or earnest Schools of Art. As a child I never saw one.
It was a time of bookshelves, family bookshelves mounting towards the
ceiling. They made an impact on living rooms but never held all the family
books. This—and my parents and two older sisters—may be why I don't
remember the impact of many books. I never did meet them. They were
always there.

At three, I knew my sister's copy of WHEN WE WERE VERY
YOUNG as well as I knew my sister, and could recite pages. They must
have been read to me, since for me literature was still spoken and the book
was really the drawings. I don't remember a copy of Lear, but while she

combed my hair in the sun my mother would coax me to recite "The Owl and the Pussycat:"

Said the puss to the owl, "Oh you deckily powl!"

I knew there was something wrong with this, as there was with the popinjay bravely born who turned up his noble nose with scones, but the rhythm forced me on. Perhaps that was an omen.

"Al-ad-din and His Won-der-ful Lamp" we all recited, in the forced tones of our gramophone record source; but "The Three Billy Goats Gruff" passed, in time, from me to my children just as I had it from my mother.

When I was four literature was still spoken, but that didn't stop me from sharing in one of my father's experiments. I was allowed to stay up for it on the theory that I would soon drop off anyway. My father had just bought a full set of Dickens: fat volumes in navy bindings, gilt-edged, with glossy full-page drawings that you could brood over. He was a fine reader and an enthusiast, and he thought DAVID COPPERFIELD might enthrall my sisters, who were seven and eight.

He was never more excessively right. For the next eight years we would never let him stop. I stayed up every night for that magical hour, while night after night he worked to and fro through the whole Dickens set; tailoring it a little to fit, skipping Victorian sentiment and clipping long, conscious descriptions. It was Dickens splendidly done, alive and vigorous, giving purpose and illumination to all books. It was also a daily family occasion, my best and strongest memory of childhood reading.

I was already at home with Dickens before I could read the older, more familiar books: SNUGGLEPOT AND CUDDLEPIE, ALICE IN WONDERLAND, LEGENDS OF ANCIENT GREECE, PUCK OF POOK'S HILL, THE JUNGLE BOOK, DOT AND THE KANGAROO, TREASURE ISLAND and the rest. They lost nothing by contrast. I read them hungrily, often following the last of the daylight across the back yard. But always behind them moved the robust figures of Betsy Trotwood and Bill Sykes, Captain Cuttle and Quilp, Uriah Heep, Miss Havisham, the waxworks lady, Squeers, Mr. Pickwick, Sam Weller. "Janet! Donkeys!" "Waller, poor chap. Drownded, ain't he?" "Try the cowcumbers, Betsy."

It was really a hit-and-miss sort of reading that a library would have tidied up. I missed THE MAGIC PUDDING, for instance. But the whole experience was broadened and extended by our set of THE WORLD'S LIBRARY OF BEST BOOKS, where I found Nathaniel Hawthorne and Rip Van Winkle and Tom Sawyer among the crowd.

There were also long, adventurous prowlings through CHAMBERS ENCYCLOPEDIA, our huge medical tome, and THE MASTERPIECE LIBRARY OF SHORT STORIES. And later (where did they come from? did we have them from infancy?) WHAT KATY DID, LITTLE WOMEN, EMILY OF THE NEW MOON and Montgomery's unfailing recipe. (How lucky we were! It might have been Enid Blyton's.) I don't remember sudden impacts, even from those; only moments of sudden understanding.

I was eight when my father gave me THROUGH THE LOOKING GLASS and turned on one of those sudden lights: the story was less fun than WONDERLAND, but it was a better *piece of work*. Both were dream stories, but LOOKING GLASS was *really* like a dream. I don't think I had ever considered a writer's performance before.

Goodness knows when or how I first came to PETER PAN AND WENDY, but at nine I reread it by chance. We were at the seaside, and there was nothing else to read. It was a shock to find how much more there was in a story than you remembered, and how the light changed as you grew older.

At ten, for the first time, I tackled our shabby copy of SEVEN LIT-TLE AUSTRALIANS and was devastated by the death of Judy. Loved characters died in Dickens too; but how much worse when they did it in a real and simple way, like people you might know.

At ten, too, I transferred to a small country school with a sort of library: ten feet of shelving in the cloakroom, sparsely filled with ancient, battered books. Here I found ERIC OR LITTLE BY LITTLE and rushed home, outraged and incredulous, to tell my father. He nodded gloomily, confirming that such things could be perpetrated, published and sold in the name of books.

At fourteen, by a luckier accident, I tumbled headlong into Shakespeare. By then I was a student of our State Correspondence School for isolated country children, and HENRY V was the play for the year. The faraway, city suppliers of the schools text ran out of copies as they regularly did, and while we waited for new supplies my mother lent me her leather-bound Complete Shakespeare.

Now that was impact; real impact. From the comedies to "The Rape of Lucrece" and the sonnets, I read nothing else that year; not even a history or geography text. There were no introductions, no teacherly comments or interpretations. Alone and unwarned I stumbled on lines like "O, he bestrides his narrow little world like a Colossus," and speeches like Mark Antony's to the Romans, which taught me construction in one blinding flash. I shamed my family by failing my year's examination and learnt more than in any other year.

At fifteen, for heaven's sake, I discovered THE WIND IN THE WIL-LOWS and pure enchantment. In the same year I discovered PENGUIN ISLAND and the dry taste of satire; and the compulsive power of WUTHERING HEIGHTS. I said it was a hit-and-miss sort of reading.

For a while after that I settled down to play the field: Victorian melo-drama tucked away in forgotten corners like that cloakroom, whodunits, the Modern Novel and Angry Young Men. None of them had the vitality or humanity of Betsy Trotwood and Samuel Weller. It became a pure delight to discover THE MIDNIGHT FOLK and Arthur Ransome for my

younger brothers, and Philippa Pearce and HUCKLEBERRY FINN for
my children, and Jansson and Hoban and Boston and Garfield and Le Guin
and Aiken and Norton...

Bibliography

THE CROOKED SNAKE, ill. by Margaret Horder, Angus & Robertson, 1955
THE BUNYIP HOLE, ill. by Margaret Horder, Angus & Robertson, 1957
THE ROCKS OF HONEY, ill. by Margaret Horder, Angus & Robertson, 1960
THE FEATHER STAR, ill. by Noela Young, Hutchinson, 1962; Harcourt, 1963
DOWN TO EARTH, ill. by Margaret Horder, Hutchinson; Harcourt, 1965
I OWN THE RACECOURSE, ill. by Margaret Horder, Hutchinson, 1968 as A RACE-
COURSE FOR ANDY!, Harcourt, 1968
AN OLDER KIND OF MAGIC, ill. by Noela Young, Hutchinson; Harcourt, 1972
BENEATH THE SUN: AN AUSTRALIAN COLLECTION FOR CHILDREN, as editor,
Collins, 1972
THE NARGUN AND THE STARS, Hutchinson, 1973; McElderry, 1974
EMU STEW, as editor, Penguin, 1976
THE ICE IS COMING, Hutchinson; McElderry, 1977
THE DARK BRIGHT WATER, Hutchinson, 1978; McElderry, 1979
NIGHT OUTSIDE, Rigby, 1979
BEHIND THE WIND, Hutchinson, 1981; as JOURNEY BEHIND THE WIND, McElderry,
1981
A LITTLE FEAR, Hutchinson; McElderry, 1983
MOON-DARK, ill. by Noela Young, Century Hutchinson, 1987; McElderry, 1988
THE SONG OF WIRRUN, Hutchinson, 1987
BALYET, Century Hutchinson; McElderry, 1989
THE OLD, OLD NGRANG, Thomas Nelson, 1989
THE SUGAR-GUM TREE, Viking, 1991
SHADOWS OF TIME, Random House, 1994
THE WATER DRAGONS*
COLLECTION OF AUSTRALIAN FOLK FIGURES*
RATTLER'S PLACE*

* not yet published

Roald Dahl

Vol. 43, No. 2, July-December, 1990

An accomplished writer of short stories for adults,
Roald Dahl began writing for children in an attempt to lure his own
kids away from television. He went on to become one of the most popular
children's authors of the late twentieth century and frequently said the
key to his success was to conspire with children against adults.
Mr. Dahl died in 1990 in Oxford, England.

$\mathscr{I}$ am a fairly old fellow and my childhood reading days are way back there in the nineteen-twenties. When I was eight and was reading voraciously, the year was 1924. At that time no household had either television or radio. The result was that in winter when it was usually too cold or wet to play out-of-doors, we had to find other things to do when school was over in the afternoons. Those things were:

1) An hour's homework or prep. Never less.

2) Making things with Meccano or other building materials.

3) Being read to by one's mother, or in my case because I was at boarding school, by a teacher.

4) Reading to myself.

Every one of us became avid readers, but there were far fewer juveniles available in those days than there are now. The only ones I can remember vividly were THE SECRET GARDEN, ROBINSON CRUSOE, TREA-SURE ISLAND, THE WIND IN THE WILLOWS, MR. MIDSHIP-MAN EASY and FROM POWDER MONKEY TO ADMIRAL (by Capt.Maryatt).

Because of the shortage of children's books and also because we had soon read all those available, we very rapidly graduated to more adult fiction, the Bulldog Drummond series, UNDER THE RED ROBE (Stanley Weyman), all of Dickens, KING SOLOMON'S MINES and SHE (Rider Haggard), all of Kipling, THE HOUND OF THE BASKERVILLES (Conan Doyle), all of Jules Verne.

By the time we were ten, we were reading all of Galsworthy, Hugh Walpole, Mary Webb, Hardy and the rest.

At the age of fourteen, I think I had read just about every great classic in literature (Tolstoy, Dostoevski, Balzac, Austen, Brontë, the lot), as well as plenty of others. Reading on this scale would be virtually unheard of among today's young people, but I did it and most of my contemporaries did it. We loved books. We were brought up on them. As a result, we not only acquired a large vocabulary, we assimilated many different styles of writing and we became fluent readers of English prose.

Today, parents who want their children to love books have two problems to contend with. First there is the ubiquitous television. Second, there is the question of knowing which books are going to enthrall and which are going to bore. It is better to give a child no book at all than a boring one. But in these days the juvenile market is so flooded with rubbishy books that it is difficult not to become confused.

The content of a children's book is basically unimportant. The sole purpose of that book is to convince the child that reading is great fun. The book must be so exciting and funny and wonderful that the child falls in love with it. Then the battle is won and the realization that books are easy and lovely and enthralling begins to dawn on the young reader. There need be no message in the book, no moral, just sheer entertainment. Not all writers for children or indeed the critics have come to terms with this simple truth.

Bibliography

THE GREMLINS, ill. by Walt Disney Studio, Random House, 1943; Collins, 1944
JAMES AND THE GIANT PEACH, ill. by Nancy Ekholm Burkert, Knopf, 1961; Allen & Unwin, 1967
CHARLIE AND THE CHOCOLATE FACTORY, ill. by Joseph Schindelman, Knopf, 1964; Allen & Unwin, 1967
THE MAGIC FINGER, ill. by William Pène du Bois, Harper, 1966; Allen & Unwin, 1968; ill. by Quentin Blake, Viking 1996
FANTASTIC MR. FOX, ill. by Donald Chaffin, Allen & Unwin; Knopf, 1970
CHARLIE AND THE GREAT GLASS ELEVATOR: THE FURTHER ADVENTURES OF

CHARLIE BUCKETT AND WILLIE WONKA, CHOCOLATE MAKER EXTRAORDI-NAIRE, ill. by Joseph Schindelman, Knopf, 1972; Allen & Unwin, 1973
DANNY, THE CHAMPION OF THE WORLD, ill. by Jill Bennett, Cape; Knopf, 1975
THE WONDERFUL STORY OF HENRY SUGAR AND SIX MORE, Cape; Knopf, 1977
THE ENORMOUS CROCODILE, ill. by Quentin Blake, Knopf, 1978
THE TWITS, ill. by John Burgoyne, Cape, 1980; Knopf, 1981
THE BFG, ill. by Quentin Blake, Cape; Farrar, 1982
GEORGE'S MARVELOUS MEDICINE, ill. by Quentin Blake, Knopf, 1982
DIRTY BEASTS, ill. by Rosemary Fawcett, Farrar, 1983; Cape, 1984
ROALD DAHL'S REVOLTING RHYMES, ill. by Quentin Blake, Cape, 1982; Knopf, 1983
THE WITCHES, ill. by Quentin Blake, Cape; Farrar, 1983
BOY: TALES OF CHILDHOOD, Cape; Farrar; 1984
(as editor) ROALD DAHL'S BOOK OF GHOST STORIES, Farrar, 1984
THE GIRAFFE AND THE PELLY AND ME, ill. by Quentin Blake, Cape; Farrar, 1985
GOING SOLO, Farrar, 1986
MATILDA, ill. by Quentin Blake, Cape; Viking, 1988
ESIO TROT, ill. by Quentin Blake, Viking, 1990
RHYME STEW, ill. by Quentin Blake, Viking, 1990
THE MINPINS, ill. by Patrick Benson, Cape; Viking, 1991
THE VICAR OF NIBBLESWICKE, ill. by Quentin Blake, Random Century, 1991; Viking, 1992;
MY YEAR, ill. by Quentin Blake, Viking, 1994

Rosemary Wells

Vol. 44, No. 1, January-June 1991

Widely known as the creator of the endearingly childlike bunnies, Max and Ruby, Rosemary Wells is both an author and illustrator of picture books and an author of young adult novels. She has received many distinctions and honors, including the David McCord Citation for her significant contribution to excellence in children's books. She lives in Westchester County, New York.

*M*y childhood had two homes simultaneously, my own, that is to say, belonging to my parents, and my grandmother's house by the sea. Both were filled with books and each in a different style. My mother would complain that my grandmother's bookshelves (which were always neat and orderly) were cold and forbidding because there were so many unread sets of great classics, twenty and thirty volumes long, their pages yet to be slit. She was right. My grandmother complained that our bookshelves were plugged and stuffed willy-nilly with all authors great and small and no one could find anything they were looking for because of the general chaos. She too was right.

Remembering my grandmother is to remember her among her books. It is to sit again in a corner of her cavernous and usually deserted living room when Sunday dinner was over, the blue haze of cigarette smoke had cleared and the decanters were still. She would be doing *The New York Times* crossword, with a dictionary, but in red ballpoint pen in what she called "the card room."

On one of the lower bookshelves were several collections of cartoons, mostly from *The New Yorker*. I pored over these for years, drinking in each Helen Hokinson and Peter Arno, trying to understand the sophisticated wit but not being put off when I couldn't. I was soaking in, without knowing it at all, just how artists got a whole world of character and feeling in to a four by five square with a few strokes of a pen.

Another book that fascinated me Sundays over a period of years was a collection of David Low, the British political cartoonist who documented the Second World War in such a fashion that it came to life and made sense to me. To this day I can picture his evil Von Ribbentrop, his clueless Colonel Blimp and his wissy Neville Chamberlain. These wicked caricatures in brilliantly clear poses explained history to me in a time when that war loomed large and in a way I have never forgotten. It taught me more than a course at Harvard. I have the book still.

I don't have any of my grandmother's complete sets. Once she caught me slitting the tops and bottoms of pages in THE COUNT OF MONTE CRISTO, lowering its collector's value considerably. She bequeathed all these sets to some institution. What I have is the memory of these sentinel books in their linen bindings keeping vigil in the shelves like distant relatives who might not be interesting to talk to but who were important all the same.

What I have also is the sound in my head of my grandmother's dulcet voice reading poetry to me against the roar of the Atlantic Ocean which lay a hundred yards from her door. If I wish to I can close my eyes and watch her place her knitting in its bag. She puts out her Lucky Strike and opens a heavy book. "I wandered lonely as a cloud," she says. The ivy clicks against the French doors in the wind and from the kitchen at the other end of the house comes the first fragrance of a German pancake she has put in the oven for me.

In my own house, which was dustier and much smaller than my grandmother's, where chaos reigned and one could relax in any position in any piece of furniture there was no end of books, dogs and different patterns of floral upholstery. If I go upstairs in my mind's eye now I find about two hundred books in my own room, all well thumbed and read many times. There was less publishing for children then and most households with libraries seemed to have all the same books, Francis Hodgson Burnett, Louisa May Alcott, Robert Lawson, Carolyn Keene, Hugh Lofting.

In the upstairs hall was another bookcase with a collection of Matthew Brady on Lincoln. In my absent brother's bedroom are "old books" meaning paperbacks. Down in the living room are at least three bookcases. In them is my father's unending love of history. There is Carl Sandburg,

Winston Churchill and an immense chronicle of the First World War. My father is sitting in a wing chair reading a book called CAPRICORNIA for the dozenth time. It is about his beloved Native Australia. He has made dinner. It is probably mashed potatoes and chops and green beans. I will be allowed a sip of my mother's beer and I will be told to finish the fat on the chops which I sneak to the dogs instead. Over dinner Daddy will tell us about the war and how it began, what might have happened if that son-of-a-bitch Clemenceau had not prevailed over Woodrow Wilson and set up the Treaty of Versailles as kindling wood for Hitler. My mother will get a little bored with this. My parents were a theater family and she will ask him to tell, instead, about Noel Coward.

Around the fireplace and on the porch there were books which reflected my mother's love of England, oddities of any kind, and anything related to her life in the theater.

There were also large full-color books with great paintings from the world's most splendid museums. I was not allowed to touch these books as a child but sat in her lap, after dinner, letting her turn the pages and talk about each painting. I can hear her voice saying, "and this is the Adoration of the Magi." I called the books of paintings "Mary books" because the mother of Christ seemed to be the most important and most oft-painted person in them. I can close my eyes and feel my mother sitting with me, a huge book on both our laps and I can hear her name the museums, "The Prado," or "The Louvre" and say to me, "Someday you'll go there!" I have, by now. But where I cannot go is back to that sofa except in my mind.

I remember a certain book which I never touched. It sat high in one of the bookshelves on the sunporch. The title frightened me when I was easily prone to homesickness if away from my parents for more than a night. It frightened me so I averted my eyes from it. The same book is still stuffed between its mates, now in my own library, high away from the books I usually re-read. I still don't like to look at it too hard and I have never read it. It is Thomas Wolfe's YOU CAN'T GO HOME AGAIN.

Bibliography

(Most titles are illustrated by the author.)

JOHN AND THE RAREY, Funk & Wagnalls, 1969
MICHAEL AND THE MITTEN TEST, Bradbury, 1969
FIRST CHILD, Hawthorn, 1970
MARTHA'S BIRTHDAY, Bradbury, 1970
MIRANDA'S PILGRIMS, Bradbury, 1970
THE FOG COMES ON LITTLE PIG FEET, Dial, 1972
UNFORTUNATELY HARRIET, Dial, 1972
NOISY NORA, Dial, 1973
BENJAMIN AND TULIP, Dial, 1973
NONE OF THE ABOVE, Dial, 1974
ABDUL, Dial, 1975

MORRIS'S DISAPPEARING BAG: A CHRISTMAS STORY, Dial, 1975
DON'T SPILL IT AGAIN, JAMES, Dial, 1977
LEAVE WELL ENOUGH ALONE, Dial, 1977
(as illustrator) TELL ME A TRUDY, by Lore Segal, Farrar, 1977
STANLEY AND RHODA, Dial, 1978
MAX'S FIRST WORD, Dial, 1979
MAX'S NEW SUIT, Dial, 1979
MAX'S RIDE, Dial, 1979
MAX'S TOYS: A COUNTING BOOK, Dial, 1979
WHEN NO ONE WAS LOOKING, Dial, 1980
GOOD NIGHT, FRED, Dial, 1981
TIMOTHY GOES TO SCHOOL, Dial, 1981
A LION FOR LEWIS, Dial, 1982
PEABODY, Dial, 1983
THE MAN IN THE WOODS, Dial, 1984
HAZEL'S AMAZING MOTHER, Dial, 1985
MAX'S BATH, Dial, 1985
MAX'S BEDTIME, Dial, 1985
MAX'S BIRTHDAY, Dial, 1985
MAX'S BREAKFAST, Dial, 1985
MAX'S CHRISTMAS, Dial, 1985
THROUGH THE HIDDEN DOOR, Dial, 1987
SHY CHARLES, Dial, 1988
FOREST OF DREAMS, ill. by Susan Jeffers, Dial, 1988
MAX'S CHOCOLATE CHICKEN, Dial, 1989
THE LITTLE LAME PRINCE, Dial, 1990
CHUT, CHUT, CHARLOTTE!, Schoenhof, 1990
MAX'S DRAGON SHIRT, Dial, 1991
FRITZ AND THE MESS FAIRY, Dial, 1991
Voyage to the Bunny Planet Trilogy: FIRST TOMATO, ISLAND LIGHT, and MOSS
PILLOW, Dial, 1992
WAITING FOR THE EVENING STAR, ill. by Susan Jeffers, Dial, 1994
MAX AND RUBY'S FIRST GREEK MYTH: PANDORA'S BOX, Dial, 1994
NIGHT SOUNDS, MORNING COLORS, ill. by David McPhail, Dial, 1994
LUCY COMES TO STAY, ill. by Mark Graham, Dial, 1994
MAX AND RUBY'S MIDAS: ANOTHER GREEK MYTH, Dial, 1995
EDWARD IN DEEP WATER, Dial, 1995
EDWARD'S OVERWHELMING OVERNIGHT, Dial, 1995
EDWARD UNREADY FOR SCHOOL, Dial, 1995
(as reteller) LASSIE COME-HOME: ERIC KNIGHT'S ORIGINAL 1938
CLASSIC, ill. by Susan Jeffers, Holt, 1995
THE FISHERMAN AND HIS WIFE, ill. by Eleanor Hubbard, Dial, 1996
BUNNY CAKES, Dial, 1997
BUNNY MONEY, Dial, 1997

Patricia MacLachlan

Vol. 44, No. 2, July-December 1991

Paul Abdoo

*Patricia MacLachlan was honored in 1996 with the
University of Southern Mississippi Medallion for her outstanding
contribution to the field of children's literature. Her SARAH, PLAIN
AND TALL, based on an incident in her family's history, won the
Newbery Medal and a place on the Honor List of the International
Board on Books for Young People, among numerous other awards
and honors. Ms. MacLachlan lives in Massachusetts.*

$\mathscr{I}$ have friends who don't remember their childhoods fondly, and some who don't remember their childhoods at all. Not me. My childhood is still with me, so utterly sharp and clear that I can still smell the smells of prairie summers, taste the hot tar that we pried off the streets to chew like gum, and hear my mother's soft voice chanting "Trot, Trot to Boston, Trot, Trot, Trot to Lynn" as I sat on her knees, my father singing songs in German as I sat in the back seat of the car as we traveled, surrounded by books. It follows me, my childhood, my past; and when I turn around it is there. And it is always full of stories; always full of books.

The earliest stories I remember, those that are part of my most hidden self, are the stories my mother and father told me when I was old enough to ask for them over and over again. My father's stories were about the prairie, the animals, the one room schoolhouse where he went to school and later taught—stories about Jack, the horse the family kept though he did nothing well. He couldn't be ridden; he was too independent. He couldn't be used for plowing because he ran off with the plow. One evening, during a storm, a frightened chicken fell down through the hay, startling Jack in his stall so that he reared up, hit his head on a rafter and fell down dead. My father always referred to him as "Jack, the horse who killed himself." There is a bittersweet quality to this story. Why do I love it? I think it is because of what it says about my father's humor and about his family, who kept a horse that was of no use to them. They kept him and looked on him with a sort of amused acceptance and tolerance for his eccentricities. My mother's stories were raucous and sweet and moving; about the depression when families came together and never thought they were poor except for money; of being chased by the family pet turkey; of a horse that always looked in the window of their Kansas home. It was my mother who showed me that I was connected to all the people in these stories; they were my past as well as hers. They were part of who I was and what I could become. But it was my father who took me one step further—into books that carried me beyond my family and out into the world.

There are many books I remember vividly. Among the first was THE STORY OF FERDINAND, by Munroe Leaf, a book I read and reread so many times that my mother bought me three copies; one for my room, one for the car, and one extra in case I couldn't find the other two. Even now I sometimes buy favorite books in twos or threes, and when she was very little my daughter asked me about a book she was buying: "How many of these may I have?" The landscape of Ferdinand drew me in somehow, and I remember making the startling connection between character and place.

The book with perhaps the most personal impact, the one that taught me about the power of the marriage of art and words was Robert Louis Stevenson's A CHILD'S GARDEN OF VERSES. I had a wonderful edition, sadly lost now, that became my world. I truly believed that I was the child swinging up in the air and down again; that I was the child in bed with the wonderful quilt on which armies marched. When I was grown my mother and I had a conversation about an old treasured quilt. "Where is that quilt?" I asked her. She smiled. "That quilt was in A CHILD'S GARDEN OF VERSES," she said. She's wrong, I know. Someday I will open a trunk and there will be that quilt, still fresh from childhood.

THE TALE OF PETER RABBIT was a treasured book, mostly because my father and I acted it out each day, some days as many as a dozen times. My father, a philosopher, educator, and existentialist, would play a fierce Mr. McGregor who would chase me out of the garden that was the living room, into the coat closet that was rabbit safety. To this day I cannot open a closet door without feeling goosebumps come up along my arms, remembering how it was to be zipped into the fur of Peter Rabbit. After the play was over my father and I would engage in what he called a "dia-

logue" where he would question me. "Say, Peter, why are you so mischie-
vous? Why are you so much trouble? Are you bored? Alienated? Then we
would switch roles, me playing Mr. McGregor and my father a splendidly
lively Peter Rabbit. Once again, when the play was over, we would have a
"dialogue." My father would ask me, "Why so angry at this little thing, a
rabbit, Mr. McGregor? Are you bored? Alienated?

What I learned from this was there are truths in fiction; and there were
choices made in books that had much to do with the choices made in *my*
life. Books were real, often more real than everyday life. Fact and fiction
lived side by side. Once, when my oldest son was very small, he was having
such a wonderful time that he stopped, looked up at my husband and said,
"Is this real?!" I know that feeling because I have cried with my mother
over the death of Charlotte in CHARLOTTE'S WEB. My father found us
and was much alarmed. "Oh," he said, after we explained about Charlotte,
"I thought it was someone real." "Charlotte is real," answered my mother
firmly.

It occurs to me that my childhood lasted a long time, longer than most
childhoods these days. Perhaps it was because we didn't have television. I
gained access to adolescence, then adulthood through books, marching
through the FIVE LITTLE PEPPERS, LITTLE WOMEN, LITTLE
MEN, Laura Ingalls Wilder; traipsing through all the books on art my parents owned, sitting behind the big living room chair next to my parents'
bookshelves, joyfully out of order so that Bible stories sat next to travel
books and Margaret Mead sat next to BLACK BEAUTY and fantasy lived
with cookbooks. All those stories, all those voices, out of twenty-six little
letters!

What I remember most, truthfully, is not one book but all books. Not
one moment, but *all* time spent surrounded by stories and characters and
places visited through books.

Bibliography

THE SICK DAY, ill. by William Pène du Bois, Pantheon, 1979
ARTHUR, FOR THE VERY FIRST TIME, ill. by Lloyd Bloom, Harper, 1980
MOON, STARS, FROGS, AND FRIENDS, ill. by Tomie dePaola, Pantheon, 1980
THROUGH GRANDPA'S EYES, ill. by Deborah Kogan Ray, Harper, 1980
CASSIE BINEGAR, Harper, 1982
MAMA ONE, MAMA TWO, ill. by Ruth Lercher Bornstein, Harper, 1982
TOMORROW'S WIZARD, ill. by Kathy Jacobi, Harper, 1982
SEVEN KISSES IN A ROW, ill. by Maria Pia Marella, Harper, 1983
UNCLAIMED TREASURES, Harper, 1984
SARAH, PLAIN AND TALL, Harper, 1985
THE FACTS AND FICTIONS OF MINNA PRATT, Harper, 1988
JOURNEY, ill. by Barry Moser, Delacorte, 1991
THREE NAMES, ill. by Alexander Pertzoff, HarperCollins, 1991
BABY, Delacorte, 1993
ALL THE PLACES TO LOVE, ill. by Mike Wimmer, HarperCollins, 1994
SKYLARK, HarperCollins, 1994
WHAT YOU KNOW FIRST, ill. by Barry Moser, HarperCollins, 1995

Jean Craighead George

Vol. 45, No. 1, January-June 1992

Ellan Young Photography

Jean Craighead George, winner of the Newbery Medal for
JULIE OF THE WOLVES, *has written over 65 books for children.*
A renowned naturalist and artist, she has camped on mountains,
by waterfalls, and even on the Arctic sea ice to tell the story
of the interconnectedness of plants, animals, and human beings.
Ms. George lives in Chappaqua, New York.

$\mathcal{L}$ately I've been rereading the books of my childhood and finding them as wonderful as ever. I am also finding to my amazement how deeply these books affected me. I am what I've read.

"The city of Calcutta," I hear my mother begin as she reads GAY-NECK to my brothers and me, "which boasts of a million people, must have at least two million pigeons. Every third Hindu boy has perhaps a dozen pet carriers, tumblers, fantails, and pouters." John, Frank and I glance at each other. Here at last is our kind of story. Real children are learning about nature as they raise pigeons, just as we were learning about nature by raising falcons.

The story of GAY-NECK: THE STORY OF A PIGEON by Dhan Gopal Mukerji *(Dutton)* was the winner of the seventh Newbery Medal, I also would learn many years later that GAY-NECK seeped into our subconscious and became part of my brothers and me. We all grew up to become nature writers, and we all grew up, like Gopal Mukerji, to write about wild animals we had raised, trained and studied in their natural environments.

The night Mother read the last page, I went to my bedroom where my falcon, a gorgeous kestrel, was waiting for me to rub my nose to his beak, and to whisper bird sounds of admiration into his warm feathers before putting him to bed. This night, I did not put "Bad Boy" (he bit me on our first encounter) on his night perch immediately. Instead, I held him on my fist, seeing not just his rich colors and bright eyes, but the web of life to which he was linked when I set him free every afternoon. Gopal Mukerji wrote about Gay-Neck's whole environment: humans, cities, jungles, mountains, predators, even World War I as a passenger pigeon. Looking at Bad Boy I now saw fields, insects, hollow trees and a migratory path across the sky. More important, the details which I found fascinating in GAY-NECK and which children are supposed not to like, kept the book alive and moving in my mind. Do I still hear that voice? I think so.

Felix Salten's BAMBI (the original, not the Disney version) came next. Since we were a family of naturalists we discussed its accuracy. I loved it because I cried from the moment Bambi's mother was killed to the final page. My father found it too anthropomorphic and gave me Ernest Thompson Seton's WILD ANIMALS I HAVE KNOWN. I dove with zest into a book beautifully illustrated by Seton himself. Here was a person who went out into the forest and lived with the animals he wrote about. He saw their lives accurately and poetically. I read more of his books. Seton's THE LIVES OF GAME ANIMALS is to me still the most wonderful of all the mammal field guides. In these four volumes he incorporates poetry, legends and science and dispels "the love of the terrible" as he calls our making villains of cougars, bears and wolves.

I grew up reading many now famous nature books for young readers including Rudyard Kipling's THE JUNGLE BOOK based on Kipling's remarkable knowledge of the animals of the Indian jungle, and John Muir's passionate THE YOSEMITE *(Sierra Club/Little, Brown),* now the gospel for our behavior in the wilderness.

If my propensity toward nature writing—a poetic interpretation of nature with a scientific point of view—was nourished by my family of naturalists and these books of my childhood, where then, I ask myself, did my child protagonists come from?

"The attic at Craighead's Pennsylvania," I answer. When my grandparents died, Grandmother Craighead's large library was stored in the attic so that we children could run through the house in the summer without abusing these treasures. Probably to save her sanity, my mother insisted we all read for an hour after lunch, which became two, three, and on rainy days, between tending falcons and pets, ten hours. In that attic amid the smell of dry timbers and old wood smoke I read LORD JIM, DAVID COPPER-FIELD, MOBY DICK, LITTLE WOMEN, PILGRIM'S PROGRESS,

HUCKLEBERRY FINN, and many, many more novels with remarkable protagonists. As I read I became each one of them, often stopping to invent new episodes as the stories unwound. When I came to Daniel Defoe's ROBINSON CRUSOE, I was transformed. Not only was I Crusoe, but I owned the island and its resources—and—I worked out a few survival tricks of my own.

I grew up, became a writer and, now circling back to those childhood books, see, at last, how wondrously they affected me.

When someone asked me the other day why I write children's books, I answered: "Children are what they read. I would like to be part of their future."

Bibliography

VULPES, THE RED FOX, ill. by the author, Dutton, 1948, 1996
VISION THE MINK, ill. by the author, Dutton, 1949, 1996
MASKED PROWLER: THE STORY OF A RACCOON, ill. by the author, Dutton, 1950
MEPH, THE PET SKUNK, ill. by the author, Dutton, 1952
BUBO, THE GREAT HORNED OWL, ill. by the author, Dutton, 1954
THE DIPPER OF COPPER CREEK, ill. by the author, Dutton, 1956, 1996
THE HOLE IN THE TREE, ill. by the author, Dutton, 1957
SNOW TRACKS, ill. by the author, Dutton, 1958
MY SIDE OF THE MOUNTAIN, ill. by the author, Dutton, 1959
THE SUMMER OF THE FALCON, Crowell, 1962
RED ROBIN FLY UP!, Reader's Digest, 1963
GULL NUMBER 737, ill. by the author, Crowell, 1964
SPRING COMES TO THE OCEAN, ill. by John Wilson, Crowell, 1965
HOLD ZERO!, Crowell, 1966
The Thirteen Moons Series (THE MOON OF THE OWLS, BEARS, SALAMANDERS, CHICKAREES, MONARCH BUTTERFLIES, FOX PUPS, WILD PIGS, MOUNTAIN LIONS, DEER, ALLIGATORS, GRAY WOLVES, WINTER BIRDS, and MOLES, 13 vols., ill. by various artists, Crowell, 1967-1969; revised, ill. by various new artists, HarperCollins, 1991-1993
COYOTE IN MANHATTAN, ill. by John Kaufmann, Crowell, 1968
BEASTLY INVENTIONS: A SURPRISING INVESTIGATION INTO JUST HOW SMART ANIMALS REALLY ARE, McKay, 1970
ALL UPON A STONE, ill. by Don Bolognese, Crowell, 1971
WHO REALLY KILLED COCK ROBIN? AN ECOLOGICAL MYSTERY, Dutton, 1971
JULIE OF THE WOLVES, ill. by John Schoenherr, Harper, 1972
EVERGLADES WILDGUIDE, U.S. Department of the Interior, 1972
ALL UPON A SIDEWALK, ill. by Don Bolognese, Dutton, 1974
HOOK A FISH, CATCH A MOUNTAIN, Dutton, 1975, as THE CASE OF THE MISSING CUTTHROAT TROUT, HarperCollins, 1996
GOING TO THE SUN, Harper, 1976
WENTLETRAP TRAP, ill. by Symeon Shimin, Dutton, 1977
THE AMERICAN WALK BOOK, Dutton, 1978
THE WOUNDED WOLF, ill. by John Schoenherr, Harper, 1978
RIVER RATS, INC., Dutton, 1979
THE CRY OF THE CROW, Harper, 1980
JOURNEY INWARD, (autobiography), Dutton, 1982
THE WILD, WILD COOK BOOK: A GUIDE FOR YOUNG WILD-FOOD FORAGERS, ill. by Walter Gaffney-Kessell, Crowell, 1982
THE GRIZZLY BEAR WITH THE GOLDEN EARS, ill. by Tom Catania, Harper, 1982
THE TALKING EARTH, Harper, 1983
ONE DAY IN THE DESERT, ill. by Fred Brenner, Crowell, 1983

ONE DAY IN THE ALPINE TUNDRA, ill. by Walter Gaffney-Kessell, Crowell, 1984
ONE DAY IN THE PRAIRIE, ill. by Bob Marstall, Crowell, 1986
HOW TO TALK TO YOUR ANIMALS, Harcourt, 1986
WATER SKY, ill. by the author, Harper, 1987
ONE DAY IN THE WOODS, ill. by Gary Allen, Crowell, 1988
SHARK BENEATH THE REEF, Harper, 1989
ON THE FAR SIDE OF THE MOUNTAIN, Dutton, 1989
ONE DAY IN THE TROPICAL RAIN FOREST, ill. by Gary Allen, Crowell, 1990
THE MISSING 'GATOR OF GUMBO LIMBO: AN ECOLOGICAL MYSTERY, HarperCollins, 1992
THE FIRE BUG CONNECTION: AN ECOLOGICAL MYSTERY, HarperCollins, 1993
DEAR REBECCA, WINTER IS HERE, ill. by Loretta Krupinski, HarperCollins, 1993
THE FIRST THANKSGIVING, ill. by Thomas Locker, Philomel, 1993
JULIE, ill. by Wendell Minor, HarperCollins, 1994
ANIMALS WHO HAVE WON OUR HEARTS, ill. by Christine Herman Merrill, HarperCollins, 1994
ACORN PANCAKES, DANDELION SALAD, AND 38 OTHER WILD RECIPES, ill. by Paul Mirocha, HarperCollins, 1995
EVERGLADES, ill. by Wendell Minor, HarperCollins, 1995
THE TARANTULA IN MY PURSE AND 172 OTHER WILD PETS, ill. by the author, HarperCollins, 1996
LOOK TO THE NORTH: A WOLF PUP DIARY, HarperCollins, 1997
JULIE'S WOLF PACK, HarperCollins, 1997
ARCTIC SUN, Hyperion, 1997
ONE DAY IN THE WOOD MUSICAL, HarperChildren's Audio, 1997

James Cross Giblin

Vol. 45, No. 2, July-December 1992

Sarah Hoe Sterling

*James Cross Giblin has won numerous awards and
honors for his informational books for young readers including
the American Book Award for* CHIMNEY SWEEPS.
He has also written a how-to manual for adults, WRITING BOOKS
FOR YOUNG PEOPLE. *Besides his writing career,
Mr. Giblin is a contributing editor at Clarion Books.
He lives in New York City.*

Commentators often decry the fact that children today spend so many
hours watching television and playing computer games, and so few hours
reading books. Whether they spell it out or not, they imply the reverse was
the case in the earlier days—that there was once a golden time when children could more readily be found sitting in a comfortable easy chair and
reading some wonderful book. Well, remembering my own childhood I'm
not so sure that's a true picture.

I grew up in a small town near Cleveland, Ohio, an only child in a
house filled with books. My father was a lawyer and also a self-taught
scholar who read widely in history, philosophy, and language. Mother's
interests were more general. A former French teacher, she read an occa-
sional novel but usually chose a biography or a travel book.

And what about me? As I look back, no one book or group of books stands out in my memory as having been uniquely significant. Instead, books were just one aspect of the entire cultural climate that surrounded me.

World War II dominated the mass media throughout my childhood. I was six and about to enter first grade when Germany invaded Poland in September, 1939, and had just turned twelve when the U.S. dropped atomic bombs on Hiroshima and Nagasaki in August, 1945. Like the other children of my generation, I listened with my parents to Edward R. Murrow broadcasting from London during the Blitz, and heard Franklin D. Roosevelt ask Congress for a Declaration of War against Japan.

My Uncle Morgan and Aunt Francile, who lived across the street from us, subscribed to *Life* magazine. It usually came on Friday, and I'd hurry over to look at the latest war photos. Staring at pictures of British children injured in an air raid or starving Greek children lying on the sidewalks of Nazi-occupied Athens, I was grateful that the fighting was far from Painesville, Ohio.

I didn't begin going to the movies until the spring of 1942, when I was eight, but once I got started I quickly became obsessed. Painesville had two movie theatres, the big Lake and the smaller Park. At the height of my movie-crazy period, I'd contrive to go to them at least four times a week.

On Sunday afternoon, I might take in an all-star Metro-Goldwyn-Mayer musical at the Lake, and I'd return there on Wednesday evening, when the program changed, to see a Warner Brothers melodrama starring Bette Davis or Barbara Stanwyck. On Friday evening, I'd catch up with whatever had been playing at the Park Theatre all week—*Mrs. Miniver* or *Casablanca* or some other popular film. Then, on Saturday afternoon, I'd be off to the Lake again for a double bill of a Western and a B-movie mystery.

Mother wondered why I wanted "to waste so much time at the movies," as she put it. But my father would say it was "just a phase" and slip me a dime for the show if my allowance had run out.

Sometimes my fascination with movies led me to books. After seeing the film version of Kipling's JUNGLE BOOK, I sought out the original story. But most of my reading choices seemed to be quite random and unconnected. I went at least once a week to Painesville's Morley Library, and enrolled every year in the library's Summer Reading Program, and looked forward to the picnic for participants that climaxed it.

Jackson Street Elementary School, which I attended, had no library but Florence Littlejohn, my third grade teacher, believed in reading aloud and maintained a little classroom library with books she had purchased herself. I remember Miss Littlejohn reading HEIDI to us and holding the attention of even the most restless students. She always cut off the story at a dramatic high point, and we couldn't wait for her to take it up again the next day.

Realistic fiction appealed to me more than fantasy, and I read Esther Forbes's JOHNNY TREMAIN—a Christmas present from a great-aunt in 1943—over and over again. However, it wasn't until almost forty years later, when I was doing research for my book CHIMNEY SWEEPS, that I finally finished Charles Kingsley's THE WATER BABIES, another Christmas present from the 1940s.

I enjoyed other historical novels besides JOHNNY TREMAIN. When I was younger, I virtually memorized all the details in Marguerite de Angeli's illustrations for her story of Quaker life in early Pennsylvania, SKIPPACK SCHOOL. Later I discovered Laura Ingalls Wilder's "Little House" books and read one after another. Later still Alexandre Dumas's THE COUNT OF MONTE CRISTO made a week-long bout with the flu almost bearable.

Among contemporary novels, I relished Eleanor Estes' stories about the Moffats and was sorry when I finished the last one. Being an only child, I derived special pleasure from reading about children in large families.

All my reading wasn't on a high level. I never got hooked on the Hardy Boys, but I couldn't get enough of the children's mysteries that Augusta Huell Seaman turned out. All I remember of those books now is that they were thick and had ugly maroon or green bindings, but Seaman's plots held me enthralled when I was ten and eleven.

Although I write nonfiction books now, I didn't read that much nonfiction as a child. I do recall one book vividly—a biography of George W. Goethals, chief engineer of the Panama Canal. Sad to say, I don't remember the exact title of the book, or the name of its author. But whoever it was, he—or she—cast a spell over me from the first page. I was right there with Goethals and his fellow workers as they struggled against oppressive heat, Yellow Fever, and unexpected construction complications, and still managed to complete the Canal ahead of schedule.

That biography of Goethals told a true story so well that I can still picture scenes from the book long after I've forgotten the plots of most of the novels I read at the time. Perhaps, in some subterranean way, it helped to point me toward a career as a nonfiction writer.

Looking back, I can't discern any clear pattern in my childhood reading and other cultural experiences. My curiosity ran in many different directions—from war-torn Europe to Revolutionary Boston, to a Quaker schoolroom in Pennsylvania, to the steaming jungles of the Canal Zone—and I followed wherever it led with the help of books, magazines, newspapers, radio, and the movies.

I imagine the same holds true for many youngsters today, and that years from now their memories of SARAH, PLAIN AND TALL will be mixed with visions of Madonna, just as my memories of JOHNNY TREMAIN are juxtaposed with the voice of Edward R. Murrow. And who's to say such a cultural stew is a bad thing? On the contrary, a child who partakes of it may well gain a more complete and accurate picture of his or her world.

Bibliography

THE SCARECROW BOOK, Crown, 1980
THE SKYSCRAPER BOOK, ill. by Anthony Kramer, photos by David Anderson, Crowell, 1981
CHIMNEY SWEEPS: YESTERDAY AND TODAY, ill. by Margot Tomes, Crowell, 1982
FIREWORKS, PICNICS, AND FLAGS: THE STORY OF THE FOURTH OF JULY SYMBOLS, ill. by Ursula Arndt, Clarion, 1983
WALLS: DEFENSES THROUGHOUT HISTORY, ill. by Anthony Kramer, Little, Brown, 1984
THE TRUTH ABOUT SANTA CLAUS, Crowell, 1985
MILK: THE FIGHT FOR PURITY, Crowell, 1986
FROM HAND TO MOUTH; OR, HOW WE INVENTED KNIVES, FORKS, SPOONS, AND CHOPSTICKS AND THE TABLE MANNERS TO GO WITH THEM, Crowell, 1987
LET THERE BE LIGHT: A BOOK ABOUT WINDOWS, Crowell, 1988
WRITING BOOKS FOR YOUNG PEOPLE, The Writer, Inc., 1990; revised, 1995
THE RIDDLE OF THE ROSETTA STONE: KEY TO ANCIENT EGYPT, HarperCollins, 1990
THE TRUTH ABOUT UNICORNS, ill. by Michael McDermott, HarperCollins, 1991
EDITH WILSON: THE WOMAN WHO RAN THE UNITED STATES, ill. by Michele Laporte, Viking, 1992
GEORGE WASHINGTON: A PICTURE BOOK BIOGRAPHY, ill. by Michael Dooling, Scholastic, 1992
BE SEATED: A BOOK ABOUT CHAIRS, HarperCollins, 1993
"Three Mondays in July" (short story) in AM I BLUE? COMING OUT FROM THE SILENCE, edited by Marion Dane Bauer, HarperCollins, 1994
THOMAS JEFFERSON: A PICTURE BOOK BIOGRAPHY, ill. by Michael Dooling, Scholastic, 1994
WHEN PLAGUE STRIKES: THE BLACK DEATH, SMALLPOX, AIDS, ill. by David Frampton, HarperCollins, 1995
THE DWARF, THE GIANT, AND THE UNICORN: A TALE OF KING ARTHUR, ill. by Claire Ewart, Clarion, 1996
CHARLES A. LINDBERGH: A HUMAN HERO, Clarion, 1997

Tobi Tobias

Vol. 46, No. 1, Winter-Spring 1993

Firestone

Dean Dinnebeil

Tobi Tobias is the dance critic for New York magazine,
a Senior Editor of Dance Magazine, and a Contributing Editor
at Dance Ink. Currently, she is working on an oral history of the
Royal Danish Ballet and a series of handmade books. Ms. Tobias is a
writer, wife, mother, grandmother, collector of vintage apparel and
housewares, collagist, and—from childhood—an obsessive reader.

$\mathcal{W}$e were in London, my daughter and I, walking down the Cromwell Road. Anne was an exquisitely ingenuous fourteen-year-old, a pupil in George Balanchine's revered School of American Ballet, and the one of my two offspring who'd given me the magical gift of reading and loving the books that had been my own childhood favorites. Pale and willowy, her fair, waist-length hair streaming down her back, she strolled dreamily along, running her hand across the tall iron railings that separated the sidewalk from private domains. "Why are you doing that?" I asked, thinking, as mothers will, of jagged metal edges, germ-ridden dirt, and emergency tetanus shots. "Posy must have done this on her walks," Anne replied blissfully, referring, as I immediately recognized, to the young heroine of Noel Streatfeild's BALLET SHOES, shepherded down this street on daily constitutionals that ended—as our own jaunt would—with an inspection of the dolls' houses at the Victoria and Albert Museum.

Instantly, I was flooded with delight over Anne's identification with that child artist-in-the-making and, beyond that, over this evidence that the flesh of my flesh was so susceptible to the influences of fiction. But then the illogic of the situation struck me, and I blurted out, "But that never happened; Posy wasn't a real little girl; she was never actually here." "Oh yes, she was; it was all true," Anne said confidently. At the same time, she eyed me warily to see if I had suddenly, tragically, lost my familiar ability to dissolve the barriers between the humdrum objective world and the ardent realm of the imagination.

I hadn't. I haven't. Nothing—neither long experience of life itself nor the encounter with more adult and exalted literary works—can diminish the power that books like BALLET SHOES still exercise over me. Today, to be sure, I can see clearly the discrete elements of its magic, yet no amount of analysis lessens its appeal. Like many beloved books for the young, it offers a scrupulously crafted, self-enclosed world. Though not without sorrow or danger, it's ultimately a world in which events and characters make sense and one in which there is a place that can be defined as home (a metaphor for safety and self-definition). At the same time, counter-balancing the prosaic and potentially stifling element of security, there is an equally forceful suggestion of infinite possibility, of wild dreams just about to come true.

These, of course, are generalities. In BALLET SHOES, as in the "Shoes" books that followed upon its success, Streatfeild fruitfully indulges her obsession with a few specific themes. For benighted souls who have neglected to read the work, I should say that it is set in London in the twenties and early thirties and that its narrative centers on three foundlings joined into a makeshift family. Overseen by a well-meaning, ineffectual guardian and a reassuring, no-nonsense nurse, Pauline, Petrova, and Posy Fossil (this is the surname they adopt) are trained, out of economic necessity, to earn their living on the stage, something they can do from the tender age of twelve. Their extended family consists of a handful of people who fall into their lives by sheer luck and volunteer to teach these "chosen ones"—without pay—what they need to know.

The most insistent and affecting of Streatfeild's themes is that of vocation. From the outset, it is clear that Pauline will make a gifted actress while Posy is a nascent Pavlova, destined to become a ballerina or genius. (Even Petrova, a hopeless misfit in the theatrical world, is recognized early on as having her own special future—flying planes.) Posy, imprinted by the fairy's kiss, is matter-of-factly singleminded, ruthless in a strangely egoless way, utterly dedicated to dancing. She is irresistible to the reader because she never has to face the two questions that haunt most ordinary mortals—often, sadly, for an entire lifetime: What do I want to be when I grow up? and its corollary, Who am I?

According to Streatfeild's world picture, which has a great deal of literal and poetic truth in it, being an orphan is the ideal condition for the budding artist. It leaves the field clear of encumbrances of all kinds. Such a creature doesn't have to follow in anyone's footsteps, waste chunks of her adolescence rebelling against the ancestors, or conform to familial expectations. She's free to become self-made. In a simple fantasy, Streatfeild embodied the concept of self-actualization—the artist's essential task, after all—decades before New Age types made so much ado about its importance. Revealingly, the sisters' "family" deconstructs in the book's whirlwind denouement. Once the support system is no longer needed and would, indeed, be confining, it splits open like a cocoon to permit the fledgling performers to embark on their careers.

Rereading BALLET SHOES as an adult, you see that Streatfeild's creation has it, unfairly, both ways. Posy and Pauline have none of the problems that plague artists-to-be in real life: They're never fundamentally at odds with the world. At no time are these characters required to grapple with the truth the film critic Pauline Kael summed up as "A good-girl artist is a contradiction in terms."

No matter how special their circumstances, all three sisters remain "nice." They're simply not permitted to be otherwise. Set against their encounter with the radiance and glamour of the stage is the grueling, endless work behind it and, even more tellingly, the cozy rigor of an upbringing that combines gentility with poverty. Between them, Nana and Garnie see that their wards never get above themselves: Schedules are enforced; behavior is monitored. Peripheral authority figures join in the discipline to ensure that the youngsters remain modest, obedient, diligent, and polite.

For Pauline and Posy, the plainness and severity of their home life serves as a corrective to the recognition of their special talents and the witchery of the theatre, where these gifts will be exercised. For the reader, the documentation of these domestic regulations offers the comfort of orderliness: The reader can escape from the uncertainties and chaos that characterize daily existence in normal life to the idealized picture of the Fossils' situation, in which one knows exactly where one stands and what to expect. Even the poverty is attractive—the beauty of making do and doing without. The same perverse magic is at work in BALLET SHOES as in LITTLE WOMEN and Laura Ingalls Wilder's "Little House" series: The periods in the characters' existence in which they have the least in the way of material resources are the most vividly and lovingly remembered.

My daughter returned home briefly after college and, since she would be moving to a miniscule apartment of her own, I agreed to store some of her books on my shelves. Organizing them with a tidiness of which Nana would have thoroughly approved, we found that we each owned a copy of BALLET SHOES, with a third to spare. This we handed on to another writer-mother/imaginative-daughter team, inscribing in it our fondest wishes.

Bibliography

MARIA TALLCHIEF, ill. by Michael Hampshire, Crowell, 1970
MARIAN ANDERSON, ill. by Symeon Shimin, Crowell, 1972
A DAY OFF, ill. by Ray Cruz, Putnam, 1973
ISAMU NOGUCHI: THE LIFE OF A SCULPTOR, Crowell, 1974
THE QUITTING DEAL, ill. by Trina Schart Hyman, Viking, 1975
ARTHUR MITCHELL, ill. by Carole Byard, Crowell, 1975
MOVING DAY, ill. by William Pène du Bois, Knopf, 1976
AN UMBRELLA NAMED UMBRELLA, ill. by Lady McCrady, Knopf, 1977
JANE, WISHING, ill. by Trina Schart Hyman, Viking, 1977
CHASING THE GOBLINS AWAY, ill. by Victor Ambrus, Warne, 1977
EASY OR HARD? THAT'S A GOOD QUESTION!, ill. by Gene Sharp, Children's Press, 1977
LIQUID OR SOLID? THAT'S A GOOD QUESTION!, ill. by Gene Sharp, Children's Press, 1977
QUIET OR NOISY? THAT'S A GOOD QUESTION!, ill. by Sharon Elzaurdia, Children's Press, 1977
WHERE DOES IT COME FROM? THAT'S A GOOD QUESTION!, ill. by Sharon Elzaurdia, Children's Press, 1977
PETEY, ill. by Symeon Shimin, Putnam, 1978
AT THE BEACH, ill. by Gloria Singer, McKay, 1978
HOW YOUR MOTHER AND FATHER MET AND WHAT HAPPENED AFTER, ill. by Diane deGroat, McGraw-Hill, 1978
THE MAN WHO PLAYED ACCORDION MUSIC, ill. by Nola Langner, Knopf, 1979
HOW WE GOT OUR FIRST CAT, Watts, 1980
THE DAWDLEWALK, ill. by Jeanette Swofford, Carolrhoda, 1983
(as translator, from Danish) THE TOBIAS BOOKS, (4 volumes), by Ole Hertz, Carolrhoda, 1984
(as translator, from French) ONE SUMMER AT GRANDMOTHER'S HOUSE, by Poupa Montaufier, Carolrhoda, 1985
POT LUCK, ill. by Nola L. Malone, Lothrop, 1993
A WORLD OF WORDS, ill. by Peter Malone, Lothrop, 1997
CRAZY AUNT ANNE FROM NEW YORK, Simon & Schuster, 1997
WISHES FROM GRAM, Lothrop, 1998

Jane Yolen

Vol. 47, No. 1, Spring-Summer 1994

Jane Yolen with her parents

Shulamith Oppenheim

Jane Yolen has been called
"America's Hans Christian Andersen" because of her many
literary fairy tales. But her output includes much more, including
poetry, novels, non-fiction, song books, easy readers, etc. She has also been
an editor of her own imprint. Married for over thirty years,
the mother of three grown children, she is now
enjoying grandmotherhood.

$\mathscr{I}$ remember certain special books by remembering exactly where I read them. I mark my childhood by the books and places. Little else from my childhood can I recall with such perfect clarity.

An eclectic reader, I was mesmerized by everything from adventure stories and horse books to fantasy epics and Victorian girl stories. But my all-time favorites were the colored fairy books edited by Andrew Lang— THE LILAC FAIRY BOOK, THE CRIMSON FAIRY BOOK, THE OLIVE FAIRY BOOK, THE BLUE FAIRY BOOK (all *Longmans Green* originally, today in *Dover Publications*).

They came in a crayon-box assortment and I read through them filled with the special wonder that fairy tales impart.

"Books Yellow, Red, and Green and Blue,
All true, or just as good as true...

went the awful rhyme at the beginning of THE YELLOW FAIRY BOOK.
Yet I was not deterred by the jangling rhythm and forced scansion. I scarce-
ly read Lang's twee introductions that dripped butter and honey and apolo-
gized in smarmy lines for bowdlerizing the tales or mixing folk and
fakelore. I wanted the stories, and stories is what I got. There were stories
from the Punjab and stories from Asbjornson & Moe's Scandinavian collection; Celtic and French sat side by side with German marchen and Japanese
tales. Lang raided the annals of the folklore societies and the fairy tale collections of dozens of countries.

By his own admission, he said "I do not write the stories out of my
own head," then admits latterly that the tales were, in fact, "translated or
adapted by Mrs. Lang." That is all the credit she, poor lady, got. It was
Andrew Lang whose name is on the book's spine and "Another Andrew
Lang fairy book, please" is what I begged the librarian for.

The color fairy books were my first (but not my last) foray into "guilty
pleasures." I would take home the book from the library at P.S. 93, the
school I attended in Manhattan, not daring to read anything along the way
because Carl Switzer and his gang of unruly boys always trailed me home,
singing out "Jane, Jane, Jane the Brain. Give me a kiss and I won't complain." (I only wanted to kiss Marcel Sislowitz, but that is another story
altogether.) When I made it to my own block, my mother would lean out
of the window of our fourth floor apartment and scold loudly "Carl
Switzer, you leave her alone or I'll have to call your mother."

I would run gratefully into our building, and before the elevator had
even gotten to the fourth floor I was deep into the first of the tales.

The rest I would read on the window seat, overlooking Central Park. I
would gallop through the stories in one sitting, barely stopping for dinner,
homework, or to watch any of the frequent accidents that occurred outside
on the 97th street crossing.

Later that night in bed, I would reread the stories, savoring the H.J.
Ford illustrations. The color plates were gorgeous, but I actually preferred
the black-and-white pictures which fell more or less at the proper places in
each tale. Ford's work was my favorite, so much so that, when in 1950
Longman's came out with a YELLOW FAIRY BOOK edition with pictures
by Janice Holland, I was so disappointed in them I could not read the stories with the same pleasure.

What made me, a child growing up in the 1940s and 1950s in New
York City, a sucker for these old books? They had first been brought out in
England, after all, beginning in 1899 with THE BLUE FAIRY BOOK, and
were full of the stories that had been told for centuries before. As any
American child living in a major city, I had no first-hand knowledge of
goose girls or charcoal burners, herd boys or sultans, groac'hs or shepherds

or any other of the old characters who peopled these tales. I knew apartment buildings and sidewalks, not castles or huts.

Maybe *because* I had no knowledge of those wonders I was drawn to them. Maybe *because* my life was so humdrum, I craved the adventures.

Or maybe, being human, I was mesmerized by the humanity in the tales. Because if the fairy stories of a hundred different cultures have one thing in common, it is this: they are simply sogged with humanity. Despite the fairies and brownies and elves and ogres and dragons and talking bears I found in them, the stories are about people and how people—the shy, the winsome, the frightened, the curious, the stubborn, the horrified, the careless and the careful—react to challenging situations.

So I read the colored fairy books at an impressionable age and, quite frankly, have never gotten over them. They taught me about honor and loyalty and truth. They taught me about courage and conviction and control. "Just as good as true" said Mr. Lang, but when I first read them they were *better* than true. They were in the deepest sense truth itself. They were about you and they were about me. They were humanity's history.

Over the years I have read a lot of folk and fairy tales. I have written quite a few myself. Some I have written "out of my own head," like THE GIRL WHO CRIED FLOWERS and THE SEEING STICK, and GREYLING. Some I have retold, like WINGS and TAM LIN. But my long and passionate affair with such stories can be traced back to the time when I sat on that hard window seat, feet tucked up under me, and—ignoring all the excitement four stories below on Central Park West—read over and over the Andrew Lang fairy books. Years later—in 1992 actually—living in St. Andrews, Scotland, for my husband's sabbatical, I discovered Andrew Lang's grave.

"Thank you, Mr. Lang," I whispered to it, oblivious to the tourists around me. "Thank you for my living. And thank you for my life." He didn't, of course, answer. But then, he didn't have to. His books had been all the answers I needed, even before I knew how to frame the thanks.

Bibliography

Poetry Collections

DRAGON NIGHT AND OTHER LULLABIES, ill. by Demi, Methuen, 1980
HOW BEASTLY! A MENAGERIE OF NONSENSE POEMS, ill. by James Marshall, Philomel, 1980
RING OF EARTH: A CHILD'S BOOK OF SEASONS, ill. by John Wallner, Harcourt, 1986
THE THREE BEARS RHYME BOOK, ill. by Jane Dyer, Harcourt, 1987
BEST WITCHES, ill. by Elise Primavera, Putnam, 1989
BIRD WATCH, ill. by Ted Lewin, Philomel, 1990
DINOSAUR DANCES, ill. by Bruce Degen, Putnam, 1990
RAINING CATS AND DOGS, ill. by Jane Street, Harcourt, 1993
WHAT RHYMES WITH MOON?, ill. by Ruth T. Councell, Philomel, 1993

SACRED PLACES, ill. by David Shannon, Harcourt, 1994
ANIMAL FARE: ZOOLOGICAL NONSENSE POEMS, ill. by Janet Street, Harcourt, 1994
THE THREE BEARS HOLIDAY RHYME BOOK, ill. by Jane Dyer, Harcourt, 1994
A SIP OF AESOP, ill. by Karen Barbour, Scholastic, 1995
WATER MUSIC: POEMS FOR CHILDREN, ill. by Jason Stemple, Boyds Mills, 1995
SEA WATCH, ill. by Ted Lewin, Philomel, 1996
O JERUSALEM, ill. by John Thompson, Scholastic, 1996
THE ORIGINALS, ill. by Ted Lewin, Philomel, 1996
LEAST THINGS*, ill. by Jason Stemple, Boyds Mills
ONCE UPON SNOW*, ill. by Jason Stemple, Boyds Mills

Poetry Anthologies

STREET RHYMES AROUND THE WORLD, Boyds Mills, 1992
WEATHER REPORT: A BOOK OF POEMS, ill. by Annie Gusman, Boyds Mills, 1993
SLEEP RHYMES AROUND THE WORLD, Boyds Mills, 1994
ALPHABESTIARY: ANIMAL POEMS FROM A TO Z, ill. by Allan Eitzen, Boyds Mills, 1995
MOTHER EARTH, FATHER SKY: POEMS OF OUR PLANET, ill. by Jennifer Hewitson, Boyds Mills, 1996
SKY SCRAPE/CITY SCAPE, Boyds Mills, 1996
ONCE UPON ICE AND OTHER FROZEN POEMS, ill. by Jason Stemple, Boyds Mills, 1997
ROCKET SONGS*, Boyds Mills

Song Books

THE FIRESIDE SONG BOOK OF BIRDS AND BEASTS, as editor, music by Barbara Green, ill. by Peter Parnall, Simon & Schuster, 1972
ROUNDS AND ROUNDS, as editor, music by Barbara Green, ill. by Gail Gibbons, Watts, 1977
THE LULLABY SONGBOOK, ill. by Charles Mikolaycak, Harcourt, 1986
THE LAP-TIME SONG AND PLAY BOOK, ill. by Margot Tomes, music arranged by Adam Stemple, Harcourt, 1989
JANE YOLEN'S MOTHER GOOSE SONGBOOK, ill. by Rosekrans Hoffman, music arranged by Adam Stemple, Boyds Mills, 1992
JANE YOLEN'S SONGS OF SUMMER, ill. by Cyd Moore, music arranged by Adam Stemple, Boyds Mills, 1993
JANE YOLEN'S OLD MACDONALD SONG BOOK, ill. by Rosekrans Hoffman, music arranged by Adam Stemple, Boyds Mills, 1994
SING NOEL, ill. by Nancy Carpenter, Boyds Mills, 1996

Picture Books

SEE THIS LITTLE LINE, ill. by Kathleen Elgin, McKay, 1963
THE WITCH WHO WASN'T, ill. by Arnold Roth, Macmillan, 1964
GWINELLEN: THE PRINCESS WHO COULD NOT SLEEP, ill. by Ed Renfro, Macmillan, 1965
THE EMPEROR AND THE KITE, ill. by Ed Young, World, 1967
ISABEL'S NOEL, ill. by Arnold Roth, Funk & Wagnalls, 1967
GREYLING: A PICTURE STORY FROM THE ISLAND OF SHETLAND, ill. by William Stobbs, World, 1968
THE LONGEST NAME ON THE BLOCK, ill. by Peter Madden, Funk & Wagnalls, 1968
THE MINSTREL AND THE MOUNTAIN: A TALE OF PEACE, ill. by Anne Rockwell, World, 1968
IT ALL DEPENDS, ill. by Don Bolognese, Funk & Wagnalls, 1969
THE SEVENTH MANDARIN, ill. by Ed Young, Seabury, 1970
THE BIRD OF TIME, ill. by Mercer Mayer, Crowell, 1971
THE GIRL WHO LOVED THE WIND, ill. by Ed Young, Crowell, 1972
THE RAINBOW RIDER, ill. by Michael Foreman, Crowell, 1974
THE BOY WHO HAD WINGS, ill. by Helga Aichinger, Crowell, 1974
THE LITTLE SPOTTED FISH, ill. by Friso Henstra, Clarion, 1975

AN INVITATION TO THE BUTTERFLY BALL, ill. by Jane Zalben, Parents, 1976
THE LADY AND THE MERMAN, ill. by Barry Moser, Pennyroyal Press, 1976
MILKWEED DAYS, photos by Gabriel Amadeus Cooney, Crowell, 1976
HANNAH DREAMING, photos by Alan Epstein, Springfield Museum of Art, 1977
THE SEEING STICK, ill. by Remy Charlip & Demetra Maraslis, Crowell, 1977
THE SULTAN'S PERFECT TREE, ill. by Barbara Garrison, Parents, 1977
NO BATH TONIGHT, ill. by Nancy W. Parker, Crowell, 1978
THE SIMPLE PRINCE, ill. by Jack Kent, Parents, 1978
ALL IN THE WOODLAND EARLY, ill. by Jane B. Zalben, Collins, 1979
SLEEPING BEAUTY, ill. by Ruth Sanderson, Knopf, 1986
PIGGINS, ill. by Jane Dyer, Harcourt, 1987
OWL MOON, ill. by John Schoenherr, Philomel, 1987
PICNIC WITH PIGGINS, ill. by Jane Dyer, Harcourt, 1988
DOVE ISABEAU, ill. by Dennis Nolan, Harcourt, 1989
PIGGINS AND THE ROYAL WEDDING, ill. by Jane Dyer, Harcourt, 1989
BABY BEAR'S BEDTIME BOOK, ill. by Jane Dyer, Harcourt, 1990
ELFABET: AN ABC OF ELVES, ill. by Lauren Mills, Little, Brown, 1990
SKY DOGS, limited edition, ill. by Barry Moser, Harcourt, 1990
TAM LIN, ill. by Charles Mikolaycak, Harcourt, 1990
ALL THOSE SECRETS OF THE WORLD, ill. by Leslie Baker, Little, Brown, 1991
WINGS, ill. by Dennis Nolan, Harcourt, 1991
EENY, MEENY, MINEY MOLE, ill. by Kathryn Brown, Harcourt, 1992
ENCOUNTER, ill. by David Shannon, Harcourt, 1992
A LETTER FROM PHOENIX FARM, ill. by Jason Stemple, Richard Owen, 1992
LETTING SWIFT RIVER GO, ill. by Barbara Cooney, Little, Brown, 1992
HANDS, ill. by Chi Chung, Sundance, 1993
HONKERS, ill. by Leslie Baker, Little, Brown, 1993
MOUSE'S BIRTHDAY, ill. by Bruce Degen, Putnam, 1993
TOO OLD FOR NAPS, ill. by Alexi Natchev, Harcourt BIG BOOK, 1993
WELCOME TO THE GREEN HOUSE, ill. by Laura Regan, Putnam, 1993
LITTLE MOUSE AND ELEPHANT: A TALE FROM TURKEY, ill. by John Segal,
HarperCollins, 1994
THE MUSICIANS OF BREMEN: A TALE OF GERMANY, ill. by John Segal, HarperCollins,
1994
BENEATH THE GHOST MOON, ill. by Laurel Molk, Little, Brown, 1994
THE GIRL IN THE GOLDEN BOWER, ill. by Jane Dyer, Little, Brown, 1994
GOOD GRISELLE, ill. by David Christiana, Harcourt, 1994
GRANDAD BILL'S SONG, ill. by Melissa B. Mathis, Philomel, 1994
OLD DAME COUNTERPANE, ill. by Ruth T. Councell, Putnam, 1994
THE BALLAD OF THE PIRATE QUEENS, ill. by David Shannon, Harcourt, 1995
BEFORE THE STORM, ill. by Georgia Pugh, Boyds Mills, 1995
MERLIN AND THE DRAGONS, ill. by Ming Li, Dutton, 1995
MEET THE MONSTERS, with Heidi E.Y. Stemple, ill. by Patricia Ludlow, Walker, 1996
WELCOME TO THE SEA OF SAND, ill. by Laura Regan, Putnam, 1996
BABY BUGGY*, ill. by Victoria Chess, Harcourt
BABY BUGGY AGAIN*, ill. by Victoria Chess, Harcourt
CHILD OF FAERIE*, ill. by Jane Dyer, Little, Brown
DINOSAUR GOODNIGHT*, Scholastic
ELSIE'S BIRD*, Scholastic
FEVER DREAM*, ill. by Jerry Pinkney, HarperCollins
KING LONGSHANKS*, ill. by Victoria Chess, Harcourt
LITTLE ANGEL'S BIRTHDAY*, Scholastic
MIZ BERLIN WALKS*, ill. by Floyd Cooper, Philomel
MOONBALL*, Simon & Schuster
NOCTURNE*, ill. by Anne Hunter, Harcourt
PEGASUS, THE FLYING HORSE*, Cobblehill
RAISING YODER'S BARN*, Little, Brown
TEA WITH AN OLD DRAGON*, ill. by Monica Valhula, Boyds Mills
TRAVELER'S ROSE*, Scholastic
WELCOME TO THE ICE HOUSE*, ill. by Laura Regan, Putnam

Easy Readers

THE GIANT'S FARM, ill. by Tomie dePaola, Clarion, 1977
SPIDER JANE, ill. by Stefen Bernath, Coward, 1978
THE GIANTS GO CAMPING, ill. by Tomie dePaola, Clarion, 1979
COMMANDER TOAD IN SPACE, ill. by Bruce Degen, Coward, 1980
MICE ON ICE, ill. by Lawrence DeFiori, Dutton, 1980
SPIDER JANE ON THE MOVE: BREAK-OF-DAY, ill. by Stefen Bernath, Coward, 1980
SLEEPING UGLY, ill. by Diane Stanley, Coward, 1981
COMMANDER TOAD AND THE PLANET OF THE GRAPES, ill. by Bruce Degen, Putnam, 1982
COMMANDER TOAD AND THE BIG BLACK HOLE, ill. by Bruce Degen, Putnam, 1983
COMMANDER TOAD AND THE DIS-ASTEROID, ill. by Bruce Degen, Putnam, 1985
COMMANDER TOAD AND THE INTERGALACTIC SPY, ill. by Bruce Degen, Putnam, 1986
COMMANDER TOAD AND THE SPACE PIRATES, ill. by Bruce Degen, Putnam, 1987

Middle Grade Novels

THE WIZARD OF WASHINGTON SQUARE, ill. by Ray Cruz, World, 1969
THE INWAY INVESTIGATORS OR THE MYSTERY AT McCRACKEN'S PLACE, ill. by Allan Eitzen, Seabury, 1969
HOBO TOAD AND THE MOTORCYCLE GANG, ill. by Emily Arnold McCully, World, 1970
THE ADVENTURES OF EEKA MOUSE, ill. by Myra Gibson McKee, Xerox, 1974
THE TRANSFIGURED HART, ill. by Donna Diamond, Crowell, 1975
THE ROBOT AND REBECCA: THE MYSTERY OF THE CODE-CARRYING KIDS, ill. by Jürg Obrist, Knopf, 1980
THE ACORN QUEST, ill. by Susanna Natti, Harper, 1981
THE BOY WHO SPOKE CHIMP, ill. by David Wiesner, Knopf, 1981
BROTHERS OF THE WIND, ill. by Barbara Berger, Philomel, 1981
THE ROBOT AND REBECCA AND THE MISSING OWSER, ill. by Lady McCrady, Knopf, 1981
SHIRLICK HOLMES AND THE CASE OF THE WANDERING WARDROBE, ill. by Anthony Rao, Coward, 1981
UNCLE LEMON'S SPRING, ill. by Glen Rounds, Dutton, 1981
WIZARD'S HALL, Harcourt, 1991
AND TWELVE CHINESE ACROBATS, ill. by Jean Gralley, Philomel, 1995
THE WILD HUNT, ill. by Francisco Mora, Harcourt, 1995
PASSAGER: THE YOUNG MERLIN TRILOGY/1, Harcourt, 1996
HOBBY: THE YOUNG MERLIN TRILOGY/2, Harcourt, 1996
THE SEA MAN, ill. by Christopher Denise, Philomel, 1997
MERLIN: THE YOUNG MERLIN TRILOGY/3*, Harcourt

Young Adult Novels

TRUST A CITY KID, with Anne Huston, ill. by J.C. Kocsis, Lothrop, 1966
THE MAGIC THREE OF SOLATIA, ill. by Julia Noonan, Crowell, 1974
THE MERMAID'S THREE WISDOMS, ill. by Laura Rader, Collins, 1978
THE GIFT OF SARAH BAKER, Viking, 1981
DRAGON'S BLOOD, Delacorte, 1982
CHILDREN OF THE WOLF, Viking, 1984
HEART'S BLOOD, Delacorte, 1984
THE STONE SILENUS, Putnam, 1984
A SENDING OF DRAGONS, ill. by Tom McKeveny, Delacorte, 1987
THE DEVIL'S ARITHMETIC, Viking, 1988
THE DRAGON'S BOY, Harper, 1990

Story Collections

THE GIRL WHO CRIED FLOWERS AND OTHER TALES, ill. by David Palladina, Crowell, 1974
MOON RIBBON AND OTHER TALES, ill. by David Palladina, Crowell, 1976
THE HUNDREDTH DOVE AND OTHER TALES, ill. by David Palladina, Crowell, 1977
THE DREAM WEAVER, ill. by Michael Hague, Philomel, 1979
NEPTUNE RISING: SONGS AND TALES OF THE UNDERSEA FOLK, ill. by David Wiesner, Philomel, 1982
THE FAERY FLAG: STORIES AND POEMS OF FANTASY AND THE SUPERNATURAL, Orchard, 1989
HARK! A CHRISTMAS SAMPLER, ill. by Tomie dePaola, Putnam, 1991
HERE THERE BE DRAGONS, ill. by David Wilgus, Harcourt, 1994
HERE THERE BE UNICORNS, ill. by David Wilgus, Harcourt, 1994
HERE THERE BE WITCHES, ill. by David Wilgus, Harcourt, 1995
HERE THERE BE ANGELS, ill. by David Wilgus, Harcourt, 1996
MILK AND HONEY, Putnam, 1996
HERE THERE BE GHOSTS*, Harcourt
LIARS BOOK*, Scholastic
NATIVE AMERICAN FAIRY TALES*, Scholastic
ONCE UPON A BEDTIME*, Boyds Mills
TWELVE IMPOSSIBLE THINGS BEFORE BREAKFAST*, Harcourt

Story Anthologies

ZOO 2000: TWELVE STORIES OF SCIENCE FICTION AND FANTASY BEASTS, as editor, Clarion, 1973
SHAPE SHIFTERS: FANTASY AND SCIENCE FICTION TALES ABOUT HUMANS WHO CAN CHANGE THEIR SHAPES, as editor, Clarion, 1978
DRAGONS AND DREAMS: A COLLECTION OF NEW FANTASY AND SCIENCE FIC-TION STORIES, as editor, et al., Harper, 1986
SPACESHIPS AND SPELLS, as editor, et al., Harper, 1987
WEREWOLVES: A COLLECTION OF ORIGINAL STORIES, as editor, et al., Harper, 1988
THINGS THAT GO BUMP IN THE NIGHT: A COLLECTION OF ORIGINAL STORIES, as editor with Martin H. Greenberg, Harper, 1989
2041: TWELVE STORIES ABOUT THE FUTURE BY TOP SCIENCE FICTION WRITERS, Delacorte, 1991
VAMPIRES, as editor with Martin H. Greenberg, HarperCollins, 1991
CAMELOT, Philomel, 1994
THE HAUNTED HOUSE: A COLLECTION OF ORIGINAL STORIES, as editor with Martin H. Greenberg, ill. by Doron Ben-Ami, HarperCollins, 1995
SHERWOOD*, Philomel

Nonfiction

PIRATES IN PETTICOATS, ill. by Leonard Vosburgh, McKay, 1963
THE WORLD ON A STRING: THE STORY OF KITES, World, 1969
FRIEND: THE STORY OF GEORGE FOX AND THE QUAKERS, Clarion, 1972
THE WIZARD ISLANDS, ill. by Robert Quackenbush, Crowell, 1973
RING OUT! A BOOK OF BELLS, ill. by Richard Cuffari, Clarion, 1974
SIMPLE GIFTS: THE STORY OF THE SHAKERS, ill. by Betty Fraser, Viking, 1976
TOUCH MAGIC: FANTASY, FAERIE AND FOLKLORE IN THE LITERATURE OF CHILDHOOD, Philomel, 1981
GUIDE TO WRITING FOR CHILDREN, The Writer, 1989
History Mystery Series: THE WOLF GIRL* and MARY CELESTE*, Simon & Schuster
HOUSE/HOUSE*, Marshall Cavendish

Comic Books

KING HENRY, Dark Horse, 1993
GREAT SELCHIE OF SULE SKERRY*, Green Man Press

* not yet published

Ashley Bryan

Vol. 48, No. 1, Spring-Summer 1995

Ashley Bryan(r.) with brother Sidney(l.),
sister Ernestine, and their mother

Susan Valdina

*An accomplished artist, author, poet, and teacher, Ashley Bryan
cannot remember a time when he has not been drawing, painting, and
creating books. Winner of the Coretta Scott King Award for the
illustration of* BEAT THE STORY-DRUM, PUM-PUM,
*he says his feeling for the handmade book is at the heart of
his bookmaking today, even though his original is now
printed in the thousands.*

When I think back to the books that meant the most to me as a child, I must include my own, uh, huh! In the elementary public school that I attended in the New York City borough of the Bronx, the teacher helped us make books of everything we learned.

Those ABC books, counting books, word books, which I bound with colored construction paper and stitched together, were dear to me. I could hardly wait to take those books home. Imagine, there I was, a kindergartener and already an author, illustrator, binder, *and* distributor of my books as well!

I received rave reviews for those limited edition, one-of-a-kind books from my family and from my friends in the community. I was encouraged. I went into full production, through all seasons, and for all occasions, making books as gifts for my family and friends.

For almost forty years I went on creating my own books. Then Jean Karl, who founded the children's book department at Atheneum Publishers, heard about me, saw my work, and brought it to a wider audience. But even if the commercial publishers had never picked up on my work, you'd still find me in my studio, happily publishing my own books for my circle of family and friends.

Of course, there was the inspiration of a world of books behind even my kindergarten productions. I'd heard the folktales and fairytales of people from all around the world. As my reading skills grew, I stayed with those books. The length of these tales seemed just right for my style of reading.

I read as many versions and translations of these tales as our library provided. I can recall special collections of the Brothers Grimm, Perrault, and Hans Christian Andersen. The ARABIAN NIGHTS, Greek myths, folktales of different countries, and AESOP'S FABLES were favorites as well. I read them slowly, savoring the language, going back over passages that sang to me, and I looked forward to the dramatization of these tales on the Saturday morning radio broadcast, "Let's Pretend."

Poetry also sang to me. I remember Mother Goose rhymes and poems from Robert Louis Stevenson's A CHILD'S GARDEN OF VERSES, Christina Rosetti's SING SONG, and Eugene Field's POEMS OF CHILDHOOD. I enjoyed the poets, played with language, and changed lines from poems over and over.

The recitation of poetry was practiced in the elementary public school that I attended. Anthologies of English verse, of American verse, and collections of a poet's selected works were in the classroom. Poetry books were always among the books I took home from the library. Each student would select a poem, practice it for weeks, then recite the poem in class and in the weekly assembly. In preparing poems for recitation, our teachers encouraged us to work for a relation of the voice to the printed word. The poet's care in choosing words for tone, color, and resonance kept us at the heart of the mystery and wonder of language. We understood that the performance of poetry, like the performance of song, was necessary to keep poetry alive.

Towards the end of each term, there were more grade level competitions of poetry recitation. Through this ongoing practice, I became familiar with poems by the English poets Shelley, Wadsworth, Tennyson, and Byron, and with the American poets Walt Whitman, Emily Dickinson, Carl Sandburg, and Robert Frost. Black American poets such as Paul Laurence Dunbar, Langston Hughes, and Countee Cullen were not included in those early years of school recitations. They were later discoveries, made on my own.

Although I was shy, I discovered that my desire to share my love of the poem I had prepared overcame my fears. I went on to win many poetry competitions. I remember when my English accent for the lines, 'Faith gentlemen, We're better here than there' from Leigh Hunt's "The Glove and the Lion" was imitated long afterwards by students throughout my school.

My parents came to the United States from the island of Antigua in the West Indies, soon after the First World War. They settled in New York City and all of their children were born there. I was the second of six children, and my parents raised three cousins with us as well. Growing up in the Bronx during the Great Depression, there was not much money left over after the family's necessities had been met. Still, there were always a lot of books in our apartment. We'd go up and down three or four flights of stairs carrying books we'd borrowed from the local library.

The library was our major source of books, and although I made my own, I longed for these other books as well. An orange crate served as the bookcase for the few books I had and I sought ways to increase my collection. I remember clipping book coupons from a daily newspaper. One could send for a book when the required number of coupons had been saved. I was nine or ten when I saw on the list books by Mark Twain, Jack London, Alexander Dumas, and a book entitled THE SKETCH BOOK, by Washington Irving. I was always drawing then, and looked forward to a book of drawings. Imagine my surprise when the book came and I first learned that "sketches" could also mean short stories. I was at first rather disappointed, but probably should have been grateful for the lesson, and for the one title page illustration in the book.

From my earliest years, my memories are of my mother singing. On Sundays, my father's boyhood friends from Antigua gathered around the piano in our living room. With saxophone, guitar, and banjo, they played music and harmonized. The message that came from my parents, without their having to say it, was that art was integral to being human, and that the arts offered us a way of entertaining ourselves. My parents sent us out to the free Works Progress Administration (WPA) art and music classes. The government had created this WPA program during the Depression to employ artists to teach their skills in communities across the country.

Because of the way I was raised by my parents, song had as great an impact on my love of language as did the printed word. I especially loved the Black American spirituals, and I wish there had been a child's book of those songs that I could cite as well as those of story and poetry. Since this great body of song has been overlooked as a source for introductory books, I have done several books of the spirituals and will continue to do books illustrating selections of these songs.

Well, if there were not children's books of the spirituals at hand, there were certainly adults around me who sang them, and from whom I could learn more. I looked to the adults of my childhood as revered elders. These elders were as living books to me, as vital a source of story as library books. I never tired of asking questions of my parents and other relatives as well as family friends. I loved to listen to the stories of their childhoods and about their adventures and experiences.

Some of these stories introduced me to the work of Black leaders in all areas of human endeavor, and I learned about achievements of Black people that in those days was not included in my school studies. This lead me to seek out whatever I could find about the cultural contributions of Blacks.

The stories of the elders and my beloved childhood books of poetry and story are at the root of whatever I share with audiences today. Childhood passes...childhood remains. The elders have since passed on, but they have passed on so much of their lives as story to me and that remains. I bring these gifts into the present. I draw upon recollections of these elders as I develop the motifs of African tales from which I work.

I will always cherish the memories of the stories and songs from the lips of the elders whom I loved, and of the wonderful books I read in my childhood. I remember voices, phrases, gestures, characters, and events, and they in turn find their way into my stories today.

Bibliography

FABLIAUX: RIBALD TALES FROM THE OLD FRENCH, as illustrator; translated with notes by Robert Hellman & Richard O'Gorman, Crowell, 1965
MOON, FOR WHAT DO YOU WAIT?, as illustrator; poems by Tagore, edited by Richard Lewis, Atheneum, 1967
THE OX OF THE WONDERFUL HORNS, AND OTHER AFRICAN FOLKTALES, as reteller and illustrator, Atheneum, 1971
WALK TOGETHER CHILDREN: BLACK AMERICAN SPIRITUALS, as selector & illustrator, Atheneum, 1974
THE ADVENTURES OF AKU, as reteller & illustrator, Atheneum, 1976
THE DANCING GRANNY, as reteller & illustrator, Atheneum, 1977
I GREET THE DAWN: POEMS, as selector, illustrator, and introducer; poems by Paul Laurence Dunbar, Atheneum 1978
JETHRO AND THE JUMBIE, as illustrator; by Susan Cooper, Atheneum, 1979
JIM FLYING HIGH, as illustrator; by Mari Evans, Doubleday, 1979
BEAT THE STORY-DRUM, PUM-PUM, as reteller & illustrator, Atheneum, 1980
I'M GOING TO SING: BLACK AMERICAN SPIRITUALS, Volume Two, as selector & illustrator, Atheneum, 1982
THE CAT'S PURR, as author & illustrator, Atheneum, 1985
LION AND OSTRICH CHICKS, AND OTHER AFRICAN FOLK TALES, as reteller & illustrator, Atheneum, 1986
WHAT A MORNING: THE CHRISTMAS STORY IN BLACK SPIRITUALS, as selector & illustrator, McElderry, 1987
SH-KO AND HIS EIGHT WICKED BROTHERS, as reteller; ill. by Funio Yoshimura, Atheneum, 1988
TURTLE KNOWS YOUR NAME, as reteller & illustrator, Atheneum, 1989
ALL NIGHT, ALL DAY: A CHILD'S FIRST BOOK OF AFRICAN-AMERICAN SPIRITUALS, as selector & illustrator, Atheneum, 1991
CLIMBING JACOB'S LADDER: HEROES OF THE BIBLE IN AFRICAN AMERICAN SPIRITUALS, as illustrator; selected and edited by John Langstaff, McElderry, 1991
SING TO THE SUN: POEM AND PICTURES, as author & illustrator, HarperCollins, 1992
CHRISTMAS GIF': AN ANTHOLOGY OF CHRISTMAS POEMS, SONGS, AND STORIES, as illustrator; compiled by Charlemae Rollins, Morrow, 1993
STORY OF LIGHTNING AND THUNDER, Atheneum, 1993
THE STORY OF THE THREE KINGDOMS, as illustrator; by Walter Dean Myers, HarperCollins, 1995
WHAT A WONDERFUL WORLD, as illustrator; by George Weiss and Bob Thiele, Atheneum, 1995
THE SUN IS SO QUIET, as illustrator; by Nikki Giovanni, Holt, 1996

M. E. Kerr

Vol. 48, No. 2, Fall-Winter 1995

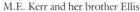

M.E. Kerr and her brother Ellis

M.E. Kerr believes that there is an important distinction between writing for adults, whose values are already formed, and for young adults, who are concerned with the basics of making and losing friends and wondering what to do with their lives. She was the recipient of the 1993 Margaret A. Edwards Award for her lifetime achievement in writing for young adults.

$\mathscr{M}$y sympathy with the underdog began with Dickens novels which my father liked to read aloud on Sunday afternoons, when movie-going was forbidden, since the Sabbath was reserved for family gatherings.

Then, on my own, I began to read American writers who identified with the outsider and the oppressed. William Faulkner, Erskine Caldwell, John Steinbeck, Sherwood Anderson, and Carson McCullers.

When we're young we often read to find ourselves, and also to crystallize a philosophy of life. We borrow glory, quoting authors who can put into words ways we feel.

I grew up a privileged youngster whose background had little in common with migrant workers or sharecroppers. I lived in upstate New York, in WASP country, where eccentrics did not thrive. My father was a mayonnaise manufacturer, whose own father was a successful chain grocer. I knew nothing firsthand of poverty, disenfranchisement, violence, or injustice.

My childhood days were spent in idyllic playgrounds of The Finger Lakes, where I sailed and skied, and belonged to The Yacht Club and The Country Club. I took lessons in ballet and tap and ballroom dancing, and learned to play the piano. I listened to phonograph records of the big bands, knitted, collected photographs of movie stars, and had only one habit which distinguished me from other teenagers. I wrote: stories, poems, chapters of novels...all about the disadvantaged and the outsider.

What was it that compelled me to identify with the underprivileged and outcast?

Some of the reasons were certainly my father's social-consciousness, and his discussions with me of the depression, the WPA, the CCC—all that was broadcast on the evening news in the thirties.

But also there was a restless inner feeling that I was somehow different, for all of my advantages...that I was out-of-step with my peers, faking my way through many of the tribal rites of the times. I felt like some Kafkaish character with a secret, who didn't know what the secret really was.

One book gave me the answer. I read it with my hands shaking and my heart beating, knowing that I had stumbled upon myself.

It was THE WELL OF LONELINESS *(Pocket Books)* by Radclyffe Hall.

I had found it back in the stacks of the public library in the "closed" section. I was an avid reader and the librarians let me wander around there, paying little attention to the books I was getting down from the shelves.

I was twelve years old and could not check it out, even if I'd had the nerve to present it to the head librarian. I read it quickly in one afternoon, and then went back and read it more carefully, piecemeal, day by day.

The year was 1939.

Until then, in my thinking, homosexuality was some sort of weird phenomenon which happened to certain males. I thought it had something to do with cross-dressing, since I had heard my mother and her friends giggling about a local merchant who owned a dress shop. He was the town "sissy," and it was rumored he locked the doors at night and tried on the dresses himself.

He often escorted a female gym teacher to parties. One of my mother's friends said she was probably queer herself, since she was "right out of THE WELL OF LONELINESS."

That overheard conversation led me to take the book down from the shelf.

Ms. Hall's lead character, Stephen Gordon, is given a male name and a male upbringing by her parents, because of their intense desire for a son. After the death of her father, and her passionate interest in a neighbor's wife, she is scandalously banished from her home. In London and Paris where she has encounters with others like her, she wants nothing to do with them for she has come to despise her "difference."

World War I gives her an opportunity to join an ambulance unit, where she can do man's work without censure. There she meets and falls in love with a co-worker, younger, more innocent and more feminine. They go to Paris together after the war, and try to build a life. But they are burdened by the ostracism of conventional society.

Ultimately, Stephen appreciates that Mary's happiness can only be realized in a male/female relationship. Stephen gives her over to a male suitor, nobly feigning interest in another woman so Mary will feel free to love him.

Published in 1928, by the formidable firm of Jonathan Cape, with an introduction by Havelock Ellis, the book was well-reviewed by the literary media. Then an attack by *The Express,* a sensational London newspaper, caused the book to be banned in England, and its publisher sued.

There were protests from such as Virginia and Leonard Woolf, simpatico, perhaps, but safely married. And from E.M. Forster, whose own homosexual novel MAURICE, *(W.W. Norton)* had been written some years earlier, but not published until his death in 1971.

The story of Stephen Gordon, and her Mary, was both depressing and reassuring. Depressing because of its dire tone, tragic denouement, and harsh stereotyping of the central character...but reassuring to a pre-teen youngster who believed that she was alone in her attraction for members of the same sex.

And within the book there was the eloquent plea by the unfortunately-named Puddle, tutor of the protagonist. She imagines what she would tell Stephen, if she dared to say the words.

You're neither unnatural nor abominable, nor mad. You're as much a part of what people call nature as anyone else; only you're unexplained as yet—you've not got your niche in creation. But someday that will come, and meanwhile don't shrink from yourself, but just face yourself calmly and bravely...But above all be honorable. Cling to your honor for the sake of those others who share the same burden. For their sakes show the world that people like you and they can be quite as selfless and fine as the rest of mankind.

Despite its shortcomings, THE WELL OF LONELINESS was a heroic undertaking, and the only book for a long time which dared to delve into the nature of lesbian relations, however sad and doomed. For most of the lesbians of my generation it was the first book we ever read about people with our same sexual orientation. None of us ever forgot our first reading of it. Often it was given to us by our parents, as a warning against suspected proclivities. And sometimes, reading it was enough to convince less robust spirits to suppress their feelings and march in step, for despite its brave plea for tolerance, it is not a recommendation of any kind.

But there it was, at least, and it must surely be viewed today as the most widely-read book on the subject...and in its own time, probably more censored, dog-eared, concealed, and reprinted than any other novel.

For me, and many others like me, it began a lifelong search for more books on the same subject. It was the cornerstone of a hidden library, my under-the-mattress books, soon joined by others like Djuna Barnes's NIGHTWOOD *(Harcourt, Brace),* Gale Wilhelm's WE TOO ARE DRIFT-ING *(Random House),* Virginia Woolf's ORLANDO *(The Hogarth Press),* and Mary Renault's PROMISE OF LOVE *(William Morrow).*

Although today THE WELL OF LONELINESS is not viewed as exemplary by either lovers of good literature or homophile activists, Ms. Hall's courage to be the first to tackle a tough subject was inspiring to me. I shall always count her book as a major influence in my writing, and in my life—my first step toward self-acceptance.

Bibliography

Books for young adults by M.E. Kerr, all published by HarperCollins

DINKY HOCKER SHOOTS SMACK!, 1972
IF I LOVE YOU, AM I TRAPPED FOREVER?, 1973
THE SON OF SOMEONE FAMOUS, 1974
IS THAT YOU, MISS BLUE?, 1975
LOVE IS A MISSING PERSON, 1975
I'LL LOVE YOU WHEN YOU'RE MORE LIKE ME, 1977
GENTLEHANDS, 1978
LITTLE LITTLE, 1981
WHAT I REALLY THINK OF YOU, 1982
ME ME ME ME ME: NOT A NOVEL, 1983
HIM SHE LOVES?, 1984
I STAY NEAR YOU: 1 STORY IN 3, 1985
NIGHT KITES, 1986
FELL, 1987
FELL BACK, 1989
FELL DOWN, 1991
LINGER, 1993
DELIVER US FROM EVIE, 1994
"HELLO," I LIED, 1997

Books for children by Mary James, published by Scholastic

SHOEBAG, 1990
THE SHUTEYES, 1993
FRANKENLOUSE, 1994

Russell Freedman

Vol. 49, No. 1, Spring-Summer 1996

Courtesy of Russell Freedman

*Russell Freedman has won just about every award
for nonfiction excellence in existence. His* LINCOLN: A
PHOTOBIOGRAPHY *was awarded the Newbery Medal and
was selected for the Honor List of the International Board on Books for
Young People. Mr. Freedman lives in New York City and writes
about everything from American history to animal behavior.*

When a friend had her first baby some time ago, I wanted to give the newcomer a favorite book from my own childhood. So I went to the Books of Wonder bookstore on 7th Avenue in Manhattan and asked if "Ferdinand the Bull" was still in print.

The clerk looked at me with pity, as though I had just dropped in from another planet. "You mean THE STORY OF FERDINAND," he said. "It's never been out of print. Do you want the hardcover or the paperback?"

He led me to a towering stack of books piled in front of the main counter—all copies of Munro Leaf's THE STORY OF FERDINAND, with illustrations by Robert Lawson. When I picked up a copy, my heart sank. "This isn't what I'm looking for," I protested. "I want the original edition."

Alas, I had been deceived by the rosy glow of childhood memory. The book I remembered—or thought I remembered—was a big book. It filled your lap. And it was gorgeously illustrated in living color. The shrunken, barebones version I now held in my hand had only black-and-white line drawings. Even so, I was assured, it was identical to the original 1936 edition. THE STORY OF FERDINAND had never been bigger, had never been in color.

At home, I re-read the book before wrapping it as a baby gift. And I saw immediately why it cast its spell on me a half-century ago. A deceptively simple storyline features mounting suspense, a thrilling climax, and a satisfying ending. It can be read easily by a child but isn't in the least condescending in either word or picture. Robert Lawson's drawings of Spanish landscapes, architecture, and bullfighting are evocative and witty. And Munro Leaf's comic narrative tells a subversive tale that I loved as a child and never forgot.

Ferdinand is a true outsider. While the other bulls charge each other and butt their heads together, practicing for the bullring, he sits peacefully under his favorite cork tree, smelling the flowers. As a boy I was delighted by Lawson's drawing of that tree, with its corks hanging like acorns from branches. Many years passed before I learned that cork really comes from the bark of the tree.

When Ferdinand is stung by a bee, his wild antics are mistaken for fierce aggression, and he is carted off to the bullring in Madrid. Once in the ring, he declines to fight, preferring to sit and smell the sweet scent of the flowers adorning the hair of ladies in the stands. Carted back to his pasture, Ferdinand triumphs in the end by being true to himself. This is one of the first books I can remember reading that delivers a powerful message wrapped in an irresistible story.

At the time, I was lucky enough to be growing up in a home that was filled with books and book talk. My father was manager of the West Coast office of the Macmillan Publishing Company. At night, Dad would sit propped up in bed, reading galley proofs. As he finished each page, he tossed it overboard. When I entered my parents' room in the morning, I had to wade through galley pages littering the floor. Dad claimed that he read a book a night.

He often brought authors home for dinner. John Steinbeck, Margaret Mitchell, William Saroyan, and other famous and not so famous, all had dinner at our house when I was a boy. They were entertaining talkers, they often looked fantastic, and they seemed to lead romantic lives, but their books didn't mean a thing to me. My literary hero was Howard Pease, author of SHANGHAI PASSAGE and other sea-going adventure novels published during the 1930s. I believe I read every book that Howard Pease wrote.

The first time I really connected books with the person who wrote them was when I was in the fifth grade and, wonder of wonders, Howard Pease came to my school. Yes, Margaret Mitchell and Steinbeck and

Saroyan and plenty of others had all been to my house. But Howard Pease, standing right there talking to my class—he was a *real writer!*

When I learned that he also lived in our neighborhood, San Francisco's Richmond District, I was thrilled. I wanted my father to invite *him* to dinner, but no luck. I guess he wasn't a Macmillan author. I remember lying in bed that night, listening to the ghostly calls of fog horns coming from San Francisco Bay, imagining Howard Pease sitting at his typewriter just a few blocks away.

Like my father, I read all sorts of books. Two special favorites were Robert Lewis Stevenson's TREASURE ISLAND and Ernest Thompson Seton's WILD ANIMALS I HAVE KNOWN, an adventure novel and a collection of natural history sketches. Back then, I didn't worry about distinctions like fiction and nonfiction. A book was absorbing and fun to read, or it was a bore.

I understand that WILD ANIMALS I HAVE KNOWN was one if the earliest books to popularize natural history to a wide audience of young readers. I haven't seen the book for a long time, and I have no idea how accurate it is, or to what extent, if any, Seton anthropomorphized the wild animals he wrote about. In terms of its lasting effect on me, however, the book's accuracy doesn't seem all that important. What counts is that I read it with as much pleasure and satisfaction as any novel or story. Seton seemed to be writing about animals as they really lived, not dressed up and behaving like humans. I've never forgotten that book, and I've been a student of animal behavior ever since I read it. Thanks to Ernest Thompson Seton, I've written some natural history books of my own.

Another book that I enjoyed as a boy, and that remains in my memory, is Hendrik Van Loon's THE STORY OF MANKIND. I still have the copy I received as a gift from my father when I was ten or eleven years old. And I remember exactly where I read it—curled up on the maroon chesterfield in the living room of our San Francisco flat. I spent several foggy summer days on that sofa, absorbed in THE STORY OF MANKIND.

The title is significant. It was a history book, to be sure, unmistakably a book of nonfiction, yet I read it that summer not to fulfill a school assignment, not to write a report, but because I enjoyed it. I read it for pleasure, for the thrill of discovery. History according to Van Loon wasn't just a bunch of facts and dates. It was the exciting stories of real people leading meaningful lives. I think this was the first book that gave me a sense of human history as a living force, and kept me turning pages. THE STORY OF MANKIND wasn't "just like a story." It *was* a story.

One other book demands to be mentioned. As a freshman in college, I read the Modern Library edition of John Dos Passos's trilogy, U.S.A. That novel, a fascinating amalgam of fact and fiction, opened my eyes to the possibilities of stylistic and structural experimentation in prose and introduced me to an interpretation of American history that I found challenging and disturbing. U.S.A. expanded my horizons. It altered my view of the world.

Today, as a writer, I keep in mind that the word *history* is made up mostly of the word *story*. Historians have always been storytellers. I know from my own reading, past and present, that a nonfiction book about American history, or natural history, can be as compelling as any adventure story while retaining the weight of authenticity. For young readers especially, nonfiction offers the satisfaction of knowing that the people and events portrayed are "really real."

Of course, I don't pretend to aim for total objectivity in my presentation of "reality," especially "reality" belonging to a different time and place. Historians always maintain a double vision—of the past and the present, trying to recreate the past as truthfully as possible, while enjoying the privilege accorded to posterity—the ability to judge and evaluate. Truth has to be sought not only by scholarship but, I believe, by fairmindedness—an attempt to measure the subject against certain ethical, social, and historical ideals.

A fourth-grader who wrote to me about my Abraham Lincoln biography had this to say: "I am very glad I read your book. I learned a lot about Abraham Lincoln, and the book was fun to read. It was kind of like a regular story."

That's a reminder of what I'm always aiming for—a regular story well told.

Bibliography

TEENAGERS WHO MADE HISTORY, Holiday House, 1961
2000 YEARS OF SPACE TRAVEL, Holiday House, 1963
JULES VERNE: PORTRAIT OF A PROPHET, Holiday House, 1965
THOMAS ALVA EDISON: A CONCISE BIOGRAPHY, American R.D.M, 1966
SCOUTING WITH BADEN-POWELL, ill. by Robert Baden-Powell, Holiday House, 1967
HOW ANIMALS LEARN, with James E. Morriss, Holiday House, 1969
ANIMAL INSTINCTS, with James E. Morriss, Holiday House, 1970
ANIMAL ARCHITECTS, ill. by Matthew Kalmenoff, Holiday House, 1971
THE BRAINS OF ANIMALS AND MAN, with James E. Morriss, Holiday House, 1972
THE FIRST DAYS OF LIFE, ill. by Joseph Cellini, Holiday House, 1974
GROWING UP WILD: HOW YOUNG ANIMALS SURVIVE, ill. by Leslie Morrill, Holiday House, 1975
ANIMAL FATHERS, ill. by Joseph Cellini, Holiday House, 1976
ANIMAL GAMES, ill. by St. Tamara, Holiday House, 1976
HANGING ON: HOW ANIMALS CARRY THEIR YOUNG, Holiday House, 1977
HOW BIRDS FLY, ill. by Lorence F. Bjorklund, Holiday House, 1977
HOW ANIMALS DEFEND THEIR YOUNG, Dutton, 1978
GETTING BORN, ill. by Corbett Jones, Holiday House, 1978
TOOTH AND CLAW: A LOOK AT ANIMAL WEAPONS, Holiday House, 1980
THEY LIVED WITH THE DINOSAURS, Holiday House, 1980
IMMIGRANT KIDS, Dutton, 1980
WHEN WINTER COMES, ill. by Pamela Johnson, Dutton, 1981
FARM BABIES, Holiday House, 1981
ANIMAL SUPERSTARS: BIGGEST STRONGEST, FASTEST, SMARTEST, Prentice Hall, 1982
KILLER FISH, Holiday House, 1982
KILLER SNAKES, Holiday House, 1982

CAN BEARS PREDICT EARTHQUAKES? UNSOLVED MYSTERIES OF ANIMAL BEHAVIOR, Prentice Hall, 1982

DINOSAURS AND THEIR YOUNG, ill. by Leslie Morrill, Holiday House, 1983

CHILDREN OF THE WILD WEST, Clarion, 1983

RATTLESNAKES, Holiday House, 1984

COWBOYS OF THE WILD WEST, Clarion, 1985

SHARKS, Holiday House, 1985

HOLIDAY HOUSE: THE FIRST FIFTY YEARS, Holiday House, 1985

INDIAN CHIEFS, Holiday House, 1987

LINCOLN: A PHOTOBIOGRAPHY, Clarion, 1987

BUFFALO HUNT, Holiday House, 1988

FRANKLIN DELANO ROOSEVELT, Clarion, 1990

THE WRIGHT BROTHERS: HOW THEY INVENTED THE AIRPLANE, Holiday House, 1991

AN INDIAN WINTER, ill. by Karl Bodmer, Holiday House, 1992

ELEANOR ROOSEVELT: A LIFE OF DISCOVERY, Clarion, 1993

KIDS AT WORK: LEWIS HINE AND THE CRUSADE AGAINST CHILD LABOR, Clarion, 1994

THE LIFE AND DEATH OF CRAZY HORSE, ill. by Amos Bad Heart Bull, Holiday House, 1996

OUT OF DARKNESS: THE STORY OF LOUIS BRAILLE, ill. by Kate Kiesler, Clarion, 1997

Lee Bennett Hopkins

Vol. 50, No. 1, Spring 1997

Lee Bennett Hopkins has written novels, picture books,
professional books and articles for educators—but poetry is his passion.
He has compiled numerous award-winning anthologies and has
generously funded two awards to recognize and promote poets
who write for children. Mr. Hopkins lives in Scarborough,
New York, and New York City.

It took a long time for me to discover poetry. As a child growing up in the housing projects in Newark, New Jersey, poverty was more prevalent than poetry! Except for a smattering of Mother Goose rhymes my beloved Grandma Thomas chanted now and then, the genre was foreign to me.

While teaching elementary school in Fair Lawn, New Jersey, in the 1960s, I stumbled upon a slim volume of verse: WHISPERS AND OTHER POEMS by Myra Cohn Livingston (*Harcourt*, 1958). The simplicity, yet extraordinarily crafted poems rang through my head. Here, a poet was relating moods and moments of everyday childhood experiences—going to the zoo, riding on a merry-go-round, being alone—presenting huge thoughts in a minimal amount of words and lines.

WHISPERS led me to delve into the world of poetry for children. I searched and found, devoured and shared works with my students by

David McCord, John Ciardi, Eve Merriam, poets who were being published in the late 1950s and 1960s.

Poetry became an integral part of my teaching career. I became a poet-
ry-addict!

For over thirty-eight years my copy of WHISPERS remains in my
library. Recently I noticed the price on the book jacket—$2.25 in hardcov-
er! What an investment! For less than the price of a taped-movie rental, I
still rejoice each and every time Livingston's whispers tickle through my ear.

In the late 1960s, after teaching for six years in Fair Lawn, I went to
work for Bank Street College of Education in New York City, in a new
Teacher's Resource Center that was set up in Harlem. One of my roles was
to work with inner-city teachers and students in West Harlem schools to
enhance curriculum via the language arts.

It was at this time I found Langston Hughes's only book of verse for
children, THE DREAM KEEPER AND OTHER POEMS (*Knopf,* 1932).
I was never the same again. Hughes began to weave throughout my life
and career.

On May 22, 1967, the day he died, I made a phone call to Virginia
Fowler, editor of children's books at Alfred A. Knopf—a naive call to
protest why a new edition of Hughes's work had never appeared since
1932. My plea was based on the illustrations in the volume which portrayed African-Americans in a most stereotyped manner.

Ms. Fowler invited me to lunch and suggested I do a new edition
culled from Hughes's adult book, SELECTED POEMS. The result was my
foray into the world of publishing—my first anthology for children—
DON'T YOU TURN BACK: POEMS BY LANGSTON HUGHES, illustrated by Ann Grifalconi. The volume received a 1969 ALA Notable Book
Award. I was off and poetically running!

In 1994, Knopf published a new edition of THE DREAM KEEPER
with illustrations by Brian Pinkney. I was quite honored to be asked to
write the Introduction. Once again the muse of Hughes perched upon my
shoulder.

In the Introduction I write: "Little could he know that more than six
decades after THE DREAM KEEPER... first appeared in 1932, his passionate, sensitive, strong, and mighty words would continue to be sung,
shouted, whispered, hummed—from farmlands to suburbs, from cities to
countrysides all over the world."

Little could he know that his mighty words touched and changed the
lives of countless numbers of girls and boys growing up, including mine, a
poor child from Newark who listened to him, who did indeed take his sage
advice to "Hold fast to dreams."

My entire professional life has been spent bringing children and poetry
together. I have always maintained that eight or ten or twelve lines of poetry can have greater impact on hearts and minds than sometimes an entire
novel can.

As an anthologist I strive to bring the very best verse into children's lives. I want them to grow up on poetry, cherish it, make it a part of their being.

When I visit classrooms I am asked why I love poetry so much. I decided to answer the question in verse:

WHY POETRY?

Why poetry?
Why?

Why sunsets?
Why trees?
Why birds?
Why seas?

Why you?
Why me?
Why friends?
Why families?

Why laugh?
Why cry?
Why hello?
Why good-bye?

Why poetry?

That's why!

What other form of literature could give me—give us—instant emotions to make us chuckle, weep, dance, or sigh—to bring those dreams to hold onto, those whispers, the melodious, mystifying, magic and might of it all?

Poets and their poems are to be remembered—never to be forgotten. Their words must live on happily everafter—forever and ever—for all times.

Bibliography

CREATIVE ACTIVITIES FOR THE GIFTED CHILD, with Annette F. Shapiro, David S. Lake, 1968
BOOKS ARE BY PEOPLE: INTERVIEWS WITH 104 AUTHORS AND ILLUSTRATORS OF BOOKS FOR YOUNG CHILDREN, Citation Press, 1969

LET THEM BE THEMSELVES: LANGUAGE ARTS FOR CHILDREN IN ELEMENTARY
SCHOOLS, Citation Press, 1969, 1974; HarperCollins, 1992
IMPORTANT DATES IN AFRO-AMERICAN HISTORY, Watts, 1969
I THINK I SAW A SNAIL: YOUNG POEMS FOR CITY SEASONS*, ill. by Harold James,
Crown, 1969
DON'T YOU TURN BACK: POEMS BY LANGSTON HUGHES*, ill. by Ann Grifalconi,
Knopf, 1969
CITY TALK*, ill. by Roy Arenella, Knopf, 1970
CITY SPREADS ITS WINGS*, ill. by Moneta Barnett, Watts, 1970
THIS STREET'S FOR ME AND OTHER CITY THOUGHTS, ill. by Ann Grifalconi, Crown,
1970
ME: A BOOK OF POEMS*, ill. by Talivaldis Stubis, Seabury, 1970
FACES AND PLACES*, with Misha Arenstein, Scholastic, 1971
PARTNERS IN LEARNING: A CHILD-CENTERED APPROACH TO TEACHING THE
SOCIAL STUDIES, with Misha Arenstein, Scholastic, 1971
ZOO: A BOOK OF POEMS*, ill. by Robert Frankenberg, Crown, 1971
CHARLIE'S WORLD: A BOOK OF POEMS, ill. by Charles Robinson, Bobbs-Merrill, 1972
GIRLS CAN TOO! A BOOK OF POEMS*, ill. by Emily Arnold McCully, Watts, 1972
PASS THE POETRY, PLEASE!*, Scholastic, 1972; Harper, 1987
TIME TO SHOUT*, with Misha Arenstein, Scholastic, 1973
HEY-HOW FOR HALLOWEEN!*, ill. by Janet McCaffrey, Harcourt, 1974
I REALLY WANT TO FEEL GOOD ABOUT MYSELF: POEMS BY FORMER DRUG
ADDICTS*, with Sunna Rasch, Nelson, 1974
KIM'S PLACE AND OTHER POEMS, ill. by Lawrence Di Fiori, Holt, 1974
MORE BOOKS BY MORE PEOPLE: INTERVIEWS WITH 65 AUTHORS OF BOOKS
FOR CHILDREN, Citation Press, 1974
ON OUR WAY: POEMS OF PRIDE AND LOVE*, photos by David Parks, Knopf, 1974
POETRY ON WHEELS*, ill. by Aloise Frank, Garrard, 1974
DO YOU KNOW WHAT DAY TOMORROW IS? A TEACHER'S ALMANAC, with Misha
Arenstein, Scholastic, 1975, 1990
SING HEY FOR CHRISTMAS DAY!*, ill. by Laura Jean Allen, Harcourt, 1975
TAKE HOLD! AN ANTHOLOGY OF PULITZER PRIZE WINNING POEMS*, Nelson,
1975
A-HAUNTING WE WILL GO: GHOSTLY STORIES AND POEMS*, ill. by Vera Rosenberry,
Whitman, 1976
GOOD MORNING TO YOU, VALENTINE*, ill. by Tomie dePaola, Harcourt, 1976; Boyds
Mills, 1993
I LOVED ROSE ANN, ill. by Ingrid Fetz, Knopf, 1976
POTATO CHIPS AND A SLICE OF MOON*, with Misha Arenstein, Scholastic, 1976
THREAD ONE TO A STAR: A BOOK OF POEMS*, with Misha Arenstein, Four Winds,
1976
BEAT THE DRUM! INDEPENDENCE DAY HAS COME*, ill. by Tomie dePaola, Harcourt,
1977; Boyds Mills, 1993
MAMA: A NOVEL, Knopf, 1977; ill. by Stephen Marchesi, Simon & Schuster, 1992
MONSTERS, GHOULIES, AND CREEPY CREATURES*, ill. by Vera Rosenberry, Whitman,
1977
WITCHING TIME*, ill. by Vera Rosenberry, Whitman, 1977
KIT, CATS, LIONS AND TIGERS*, ill. by Vera Rosenberry, Whitman, 1978
MERRILY COMES OUR HARVEST IN: POEMS FOR THANKSGIVING*, ill. by Ben
Schecter, Harcourt, 1978; Boyds Mills, 1993
TO LOOK AT ANY THING*, photos by John Earl, Harcourt, 1978
EASTER BUDS ARE SPRINGING: POEMS FOR EASTER*, ill. by Tomie dePaola, Harcourt,
1979; Boyds Mills, 1993
GO TO BED! A BOOK OF BEDTIME POEMS*, ill. by Rosekrans Hoffman, Knopf, 1979
MERELY PLAYERS: AN ANTHOLOGY OF LIFE POEMS*, Elsevier/Nelson, 1979
MY MANE CATCHES THE WIND: POEMS ABOUT HORSES*, ill. by Sam Savitt,
Harcourt, 1979
PUPS, DOGS, FOXES AND WOLVES*, ill. by Vera Rosenberry, Whitman, 1979
WONDER WHEELS, (novel), Knopf, 1979
THE BEST OF BOOK BONANZA, Holt, 1980
BY MYSELF*, ill. by Glo Coalson, Crowell, 1980

ELVES, FAIRIES, & GNOMES*, ill. by Rosekrans Hoffman, Knopf, 1980
MOMENTS: POEMS ABOUT THE SEASONS*, ill. by Michael Hague, Harcourt, 1980
MORNING, NOON, AND NIGHTTIME*, TOO, ill. by Nancy Hannans, Harper, 1980
I AM THE CAT*, ill. by Linda Rochester Richards, Harcourt, 1981
MAMA AND HER BOYS: A NOVEL, Harper, 1981; ill. by Stephen Marchese, Simon & Schuster, 1993
AND GOD BLESS ME: PRAYERS, LULLABIES AND DREAM-POEMS*, ill. by Patricia Henderson Lincoln, Knopf, 1982
CIRCUS! CIRCUS!*, ill. by John O'Brien, Knopf, 1982
RAINBOWS ARE MADE: POEMS BY CARL SANDBURG*, ill. by Fritz Eichenberg, Harcourt, 1982
A DOG'S LIFE*, ill. by Linda Rochester Richards, Harcourt, 1983
HOW DO YOU MAKE AN ELEPHANT FLOAT? AND OTHER DELICIOUS RIDDLES, ill. by Rosekrans Hoffman, Whitman, 1983
THE SKY IS FULL OF SONG*, ill. by Dirk Zimmer, Harper, 1983
A SONG IN STONE: CITY POEMS*, photos by Anna Held Audette, Crowell, 1983
CRICKETS AND BULLFROGS AND WHISPERS OF THUNDER: POEMS AND PICTURES BY HARRY BEHN*, Harcourt, 1984
LOVE & KISSES*, ill. by Kris Boyd, Houghton, 1984
SURPRISES*, ill. by Megan Lloyd, Harper, 1984
CREATURES*, ill. by Stella Ormai, Harcourt, 1985
MUNCHING: POEMS ABOUT FOOD AND EATING*, ill. by Nelle Davis, Little, Brown, 1985
BEST FRIENDS*, ill. by James Watts, Harper, 1986
THE SEA IS CALLING ME*, ill. by Walter Gaffney-Kessell, Harcourt, 1986
DINOSAURS*, ill. by Murray Tinkelman, Harcourt, 1987
CLICK, RUMBLE, ROAR: POEMS ABOUT MACHINES*, ill. by Anna Held Audette, Crowell, 1987
MORE SURPRISES*, ill. by Megan Lloyd, Harper, 1987
SIDE BY SIDE: POEMS TO READ TOGETHER*, ill. by Hilary Knight, Simon & Schuster, 1988
VOYAGES: POEMS BY WALT WHITMAN*, ill. by Charles Mikolaycak, Harcourt, 1988
ANIMALS FROM MOTHER GOOSE: A QUESTION BOOK, ill. by Kathryn Hewitt, Harcourt, 1989
PEOPLE FROM MOTHER GOOSE: A QUESTION BOOK, ill. by Kathryn Hewitt, Harcourt, 1989
STILL AS A STAR: A BOOK OF NIGHTTIME POEMS*, ill. by Karen Milone, Little, Brown, 1989
GOOD BOOKS, GOOD TIMES!*, ill. by Harvey Stevenson, HarperCollins, 1990
HAPPY BIRTHDAY*, ill. by Hilary Knight, Simon & Schuster, 1991
ON THE FARM*, ill. by Laurel Molk, Little, Brown, 1991
FLIT, FLUTTER, FLY! POEMS ABOUT BUGS AND OTHER CRAWLY CREATURES*, ill. by Peter Palagonia, Doubleday, 1992
QUESTIONS*, ill. by Carolyn Croll, HarperCollins, 1992
RING OUT, WILD BELLS: POEMS ABOUT HOLIDAYS AND SEASONS*, ill. by Karen Baumann, Harcourt, 1992
THROUGH OUR EYES: POEMS AND PICTURES ABOUT GROWING UP*, ill. by Jeffrey Dunn, Little, Brown, 1992
TO THE ZOO: ANIMAL POEMS*, ill. by John Wallner, Little, Brown, 1992
EXTRA INNINGS: BASEBALL POEMS*, ill. by Scott Medlock, Harcourt, 1993
IT'S ABOUT TIME!*, ill. by Matt Novak, Simon & Schuster, 1993
RAGGED SHADOWS: POEMS OF HALLOWEEN NIGHT*, ill. by Giles Laroche, Little, Brown, 1993
BEEN TO YESTERDAYS: POEMS OF A LIFE, Boyds Mills, 1995
BLAST OFF! POEMS ABOUT SPACE*, ill. by Melissa Sweet, HarperCollins, 1995
GOOD RHYMES, GOOD TIMES, ill. by Frané Lessac, HarperCollins, 1995
PAUSES: AUTOBIOGRAPHICAL REFLECTIONS OF 101 CREATORS OF CHILDREN'S BOOKS, HarperCollins, 1995
SMALL TALK: A BOOK OF SHORT POEMS*, ill. by Susan Gaber, Harcourt, 1995
OPENING DAYS: SPORTS POEMS*, ill. by Scott Medlock, Harcourt, 1996
SCHOOL SUPPLIES: A BOOK OF POEMS*, ill. by Renée Flower, Simon & Schuster, 1996

SONG AND DANCE*, ill. Cheryl Munro Taylor, Simon & Schuster, 1997
MARVELOUS MATH: A BOOK OF POEMS*, ill. by Karen Barbout, Simon & Schuster, 1997

* anthology